The Leisure Suit LARRY™ Story

Mueller
Schuchardt

Abacus

A Data Becker Book

Mueller/Schuchardt

The

Leisure Suit

Larry

Story

ABACUS
DATA BECKER

Foreword

You're about to embark on a journey into funland. You're going to have some of the best fun possible in the computer age. You're going on an adventure with Larry Laffer.

In this book you'll read all about Larry, discover who he is and what his strengths and weaknesses are. You'll read all about his adventures and learn how to save him (and yourself) from the clutches of fate.

Maybe you already have friends who play Leisure Suit Larry. Talk to them and ask them for solutions to problems you've encountered when playing the Leisure Suit Larry games. We're speaking from experience. While writing this book, we ran up some pretty high phone bills asking for help. But we had a lot of fun renewing old friendships and making new friends along the way.

We've tried to take the characteristics of the Leisure Suit Larry games into account. Don't expect a methodical, detailed introduction into the world of the Leisure Suit Larry games with answers to all of your questions.

Please understand that Sierra On-Line intends the Leisure Suit Larry series to be humorous, harmless endeavors for adults only. Parents should carefully consider whether these games should be played by children.

This book is divided into four parts:

In the first part you'll find some pointers on how to find your way around Larry's world. There is a description of Larry's language, an introduction to Larry's grammar and a partial list of Larry's vocabulary.

In the second part you'll find a summary of the entire Leisure Suit Larry Series. We tried to give as little information as possible on solutions to Larry's problems, so that you'll still have fun and adventure when finding your own solutions to the games.

Read the third part of the book carefully: It contains the solutions for all three Leisure Suit Larry games. You can look at this part of the book on those late nights (or early mornings) when you just can't go any farther in the games.

We figured this would be a lot better than calling up your friends at 2:00 in the morning to ask them a question about Leisure Suit Larry.

The fourth part is more technical. There are detailed instructions for installing the game programs on any system, whether it's an IBM compatible PC, an Atari ST, a Commodore Amiga or even a Macintosh.

The following Leisure Suit Larry games are available
(as of January 1990, published by Sierra):

Game	IBM PC/AT	Atari ST	Amiga	MAC
Larry 1	Yes	Yes	Yes	Yes
The Land of the Lounge Lizards				
Larry 2	Yes	Yes	Yes	3rd. Qtr. 90
Looking for Love (in Several Wrong Places)				
Larry 3	Yes	1st. Qtr. 90	–	4th. Qtr. 90
Passionate Patti in Pursuit of the Pulsating Pectorals				

Table of Contents

1. Game Tips

Before discussing the game itself, we'll present some general tips for playing the Leisure Suit Larry games. First, we'll show you how to move the main character, Larry, through the adventure and how to get out of tricky situations. However, we cannot avoid discussing some of the less exciting details of playing the Leisure Suit Larry games.

In the second part of this chapter, we'll explain the language used in the games.

The playing area

Note: This section contains a description of how to play the Leisure Suit Larry games on a PC. Any differences that might occur with different computer systems are discussed in Chapter 6.

The Way through the Larry games

The object of all Leisure Suit Larry games is to move the figure, Larry, through various scenes in order to attain an objective, which is unknown to the player at the beginning of the game. Using the computer keyboard, you command the figure to perform certain actions. You can usually tell whether an action is successful by an increase in the points displayed in the upper screen border.

First, you must move the Larry figure. You can move him either with the cursor keys or (beginning with Larry 2) with the mouse. Larry can only move in eight directions: right and left, up and down. The other four directions are situated between these four main directions, similar to a compass.

The easiest way to move in these directions is with the help of the cursor keys located on the numeric keypad of your keyboard. Using the example of the compass, "North" = <8>, "Northeast" = <9>, "East" = <6>, "Southeast" = <3>, "South" = <2>, "Southwest" = <1>, "West" = <4> and "Northwest" = <7>. The center key, <5> stops movement. To stop any movement press the direction key twice. Otherwise, regardless of which direction Larry moves, he will eventually stop because he'll run into a wall or a tree. Larry might even fall off a cliff.

Many players prefer using the mouse to move the figure. To do this, simply place the mouse pointer on the side of the figure that points to the direction you want him to move and press the left mouse button. The figure will only move in the direction closest to the one you specified with the mouse pointer.

Basically, Larry cannot go through walls or obstacles. If something is in the way, he must go around it. When the figure reaches the screen border, there are two possibilities: Either Larry continues to the next screen or the game is over. Since some of the passageways are well hidden, you should try to get to the next screen from different places on the screen.

Commands

Enter all the other commands by simply typing them on the keyboard. The only time you cannot immediately enter a command is when the program displays a message on the screen. These messages are your only chance to obtain tips from the program, so read them carefully. Once you've read the message, press <Enter> to continue with the program.

Many scenes are programmed to run without giving you a chance to enter any commands. In this instance, the only thing you can do is wait for the end of the scene. You'll know that the scene is over when the figure starts responding to the cursor keys or the mouse again. After entering the command, simply press <Enter> and wait for the program to react. If you make a mistake while entering the command, the program will give you a more or less friendly reminder. Since the error messages become more rude with each new Larry sequel, one may wonder what Larry 8 will be like.

You don't have to re-enter the entire command if you mistakenly type an incorrect letter. By pressing <F3> you can repeat the last command that was entered. The command containing the incorrect letter will then appear in the entry line, where you can correct it. In Larry 1, you can also use the

<Backspace> key to go back to the mistake, correct it and complete the command. Starting with Larry 2, you can move the cursor within the last entered command, which allows you to correct mistakes more quickly. The <Space bar> or <F3> can be used to repeat the last command.

When you enter a new scene, type "Look" so that you can take a look around. Once this command is entered, a general description of the scenery surrounding the character will be displayed. This is especially useful for players who have installed Larry on a PC with a monochrome graphic adapter. Since the capabilities of graphic cards are limited, typing "Look" enables you to determine, for example, whether you're looking at a television or a cigarette machine.

Inspect all of the objects in the new scene very carefully. Especially notice the objects that the program voluntarily mentions after you entered "Look". For example, if you are looking at a PC, move close to it and enter "Look at PC". You may receive more information on the PC. Keep in mind that the information may or may not help you. Either way, you may have fun with the answer.

A second, third or even fourth look can often be very rewarding. Just repeat the last command ("Look at PC") by pressing <F3> or the <Space bar>. Occasionally you will receive a different answer than the previous time. To find out how many different answers there are, repeat the last command until you get the same answer twice. Then you'll have all available information on the object.

You can also use this method in different situations. For example, to talk to another figure (usually a girl), enter "talk to girl". To continue the conversation, repeat the command until the girl becomes bored and repeats her answers. This is a sure sign that the figure has said everything that it can.

Sometimes when entering a command you won't receive the answer you had expected. For example, the program might refuse to execute a certain action. Press <F3> or the <Space bar> to repeat your command.

Inventory

All of the actions Larry performs are for the purpose of getting various objects that he can use to achieve his goal.

Each of the three games contains an option that enables you to keep track of your equipment. When <Tab> is pressed a list of everything that Larry is carrying appears on the screen. You'll be amazed at the amount of objects that can fit into Larry's pocket. Just remember, since it's only a game, anything is possible.

However, simply studying this list isn't always sufficient. You can also use "Look" to get a closer look at any of the objects that Larry has. For example, to discover what Larry has in his wallet, enter "Look at wallet".

After the second version of Larry, you don't have to use "Look at..." to see what Larry is carrying with him. Simply press <Tab> once to see a list of all available equipment. Press <Tab> a second time to highlight the first object. For a closer look at the object, press <Enter> and all of the available information about the object will be displayed. Press <Tab> again to move to the next object. Continue to press <Tab> until you reach the object you want to study and then press <Enter>.

Not all of the information you receive is interesting or meaningful. You can decide whether it's funny.

Saving games

As we know, adventurers live dangerously. This also applies to Larry, even though he isn't exactly an adventurer. Every step he takes and every action he performs can be fatal. Since Larry only exists in the memory of your computer, this doesn't matter to him. After all, you can always start up the computer again. However, entering the same commands over and over again, just to avoid making a mistake on your second try, can become tedious.

Larry is also a time-consuming game. Even computer game experts won't be able to play a complete Larry game in one evening. That's not the purpose of the game. Since the developers of Larry understood this, they gave players the option of saving the score and continuing the game at some other time.

If you believe that your Larry figure will soon encounter a disaster or that you may need a couple of hours sleep before going to work in the morning, enter "Save game". The program will then prompt you for the name under which your current score will be saved. You're not limited to DOS conventions (eight letters plus a three letter extension). The program provides its own filenames. Use a name that identifies the current game you're playing.

Use "restore game" to continue from where you stopped. The program will then display a list of all saved scores. Choose your score and continue playing. "Save game" or "restore game" don't have to be used all of the time. You can also press <F5> to save the game or <F7> to restore it.

As we previously mentioned, Larry is constantly in danger of making a fatal, false step. So, you should save your score on a regular basis. Beginning with Larry 3, the program reminds you every five minutes that it's time to save. However, in Larry 1 and Larry 2 you must remember to save on your own. This process guarantees that you won't lose more than five minutes of typing. However, this doesn't mean that you are completely safe by saving every five minutes. Since the games have such a complex structure you can make a mistake and not notice it until it comes back to haunt you much later.

However, there are provisions for this situation; it's possible to save not one, but twelve scores. Fully utilize this option and set up new files to store the scores on a regular basis. When all twelve files, which the function "save - restore" manages, are full, you can use one of two options. Either overwrite one of the files or change to a different subdirectory. What you do depends on your personal preference.

Other Functions of the User Interface

Besides the option of saving a score and calling it again, there are also other functions of the user interface. All of the functions of the user interface are hidden in a menu located on the top screen border. You can activate this menu at any time by pressing <Esc> or by using the mouse. Use the cursor keys to open the windows of the menu.

New functions have been added to the menu in the sequels to Leisure Suit Larry. We will discuss the functions in order, from Larry 1 to the most recent version.

The menu line in Larry 1 has five menus. The newer versions also have five menus, but changes have been made on those five menus. In Larry 1 the five menus are "Sierra", "File", "Action", "Special" and "Speed". The menus operate similar to a GEM or Macintosh operating system. The first menu on the left provides general information about the program. The next window contains all of the different functions related to files, loading, saving or ending the program. Next are the menu windows that apply to the program itself.

Let's begin on the left. In the menu "Sierra", under "About Larry", there is information about the game and its programmers. Then there is "Help", which offers helpful information about playing the game. You can also press <F1> for help. Don't expect too much from this "helpful information" however. The last two points in the "Sierra" menu provide some amazing additional functions: "Calculator" contains some fascinating information about combinations of small, even numbers, while "Puzzle" contains a puzzle that is entertaining, but doesn't have anything to do with the game. The next menu window is called "File". As we mentioned, this is where all of the file management occurs: saving games ("save game" <F5>), restoring saved games ("restore game" <F7>), restarting ("restart game" <F9>) and finally, leaving the program ("quit" <Alt><Z>).

The next menu is called "Action". The functions of this menu are related to the course of the game itself. The first point is "inventory" (<Tab>). The next point, "see object", is directly related to the first point. When you select this function, a list of all of the objects that Larry is carrying with him, will appear. You can select any object that interests you and get a closer look. The last point in the "Action" menu was discontinued in the later versions. It is called "Bodily Function" and allows you to choose whether he should "breathe", "belch" or "fart". You can make up new bodily functions like "frettle", and see how they influence the course of the game.

The fourth window, "Special", provides a wide spectrum of functions. Press <F2> to get the function "Sound on/off", which you can use to turn your computer loudspeaker on or off. We guarantee that, sooner or later, you'll get sick and tired of the music that accompanies Leisure Suit Larry. Press <Ctrl><J> to get "Joystick", which gives you control over the joystick. Use "Clock on/off" to display the current time during the game.

Of course you can't have a computer game without a "boss key". To obtain the boss key in Leisure Suit Larry games, press <Ctrl><B>. This is also displayed in the "Special" menu. However, use the boss key with caution. First of all, your boss must be really naive if he believes that this display is part of your normal work and secondly, you must be prepared to lose your current score after you press the boss key. Once this happens you can either start the game over with <F9>, or call the last game you saved, with <F7>, if you saved a game.

To give you a chance to grab a beer or a soda from the refrigerator, the menu "Special" also contains the "Pause Game" function. Just press "Pause Game", get your drink, and press <Enter> to continue where you left off. In Leisure Suit Larry 1, you can also press <Esc> to pause.

The last window in the main menu of Leisure Suit Larry 1 is called "Speed". You can play Larry 1 in four different speeds: "Normal", "Slow", "Fast" and

"Fastest". To change speeds, either call "Speed" or press <F10> to switch to the next speed. Remember that Leisure Suit Larry isn't a video game, in which the faster you play the more points you gain. The purpose of the four speeds is to adjust the game to the speed of your computer. On a PC, you usually have to speed up Larry, while on a 386 you will have to slow him down.

This concludes our discussion of Leisure Suit Larry 1. The menus of the two newer versions of Larry are basically the same. The only difference in the second version of Larry is that the points under "Special" have been added to "Action" and "Sound" replaced "Special".

The "Sierra" menu has been replaced by the Sierra logo. Under the logo you'll find a window containing general information about the game ("About LSL2/ 3" - <Ctrl><A>) and helpful information ("Help" - <F1>). The functions

"Calculator" and "Puzzle" were phased out. The "File" menu is the same as in Leisure Suit Larry 1, except now you use <Ctrl><Q> instead of <Alt><Z> to quit. In Leisure Suit Larry 3 one option has been added to the "File" menu. You can have the computer remind you to save your scores at regular intervals. To set these intervals, call "Auto Save" by pressing <F4>. The standard setting is five minutes.

The next menu is called "Action". You will find the points "Pause Game" (<Ctrl><P>), "Inventory" (<Ctrl><I>), "Retype" (<F3> or the <Space bar>), and "Boss key" (<Ctrl><B>).

In Leisure Suit Larry 2, the "Filth Level" (<Ctrl><F>) was added. You can choose your own setting for this. Filth level has no effect on the game itself. Larry 2 also includes "Trite Phrase". In Larry's second adventure he is surrounded by nice people who constantly tell him, "Have a nice day". If the phrase "Have a nice day" starts to get on your nerves, you can set another trite phrase, such as "God bless you".

Life has gotten a lot harder for Larry in his third adventure. Instead of greeting Larry with trite phrases, people swear at him instead. If you get bored with "Damn", you can change it in the "Action" menu or by pressing <Ctrl><X> to something else. For example, you could use the Cockney term "Blimey", or even "Son of a bitch".

The filth level in Leisure Suit Larry 3 contains more foul language than Larry 2. We'll discuss this later. Larry 3 enables you to change the color of the screen. The standard setting is blue writing on a white background. To change colors, select "Colors" in the "Action" menu, or press <Ctrl><C>. The program will prompt you for a number between zero and fifteen. You can use any setting you want as long as the letters and the background are different colors. After all, you are supposed to be able to see it.

Number codes for text and background color:			
0	Black	8	Dark Grey
1	Blue	9	Light Blue
2	Green	10	Light Green
3	Turquoise	11	Light Turquoise
4	Red	12	Light Red
5	Purple	13	Light Purple
6	Brown	14	Yellow
7	Light Grey	15	White

After the "Action" menu there is "Speed". You can set the speed the same way you did in Larry 1, except for one difference. In Leisure Suit Larry 2 and 3 you can choose among fifteen different settings. You can either set a speed under "Change", in the "Speed" menu, or with <Ctrl><S>. You can also select "Slower", "Faster" or "Normal" in the menu. The easiest way to change speeds is to press <+>, <->, or <=>; these keys can be pressed while you're playing the game.

The last menu window of Leisure Suit Larry 2 and 3 is called "Sound". You can use this to turn on/off the sound of the Larry game. We will discuss sound in more detail at the end of the book.

Larry's language

Larry only understands American English. International Larry fans should carefully read the vocabulary listed in the next section.

The Grammar

The grammar is quite simple in Larry games. Whether this proves that Larry is simple is another matter. Larry simply wants success and a comfortable life. Although we all want these things, Larry wants them right away, unlike the rest of us (we won't admit it).

Now back to the grammar. All of the entries that you make will be commands. Don't use complete sentences such as, "Larry, please enter the cab." because you will only receive an error message from the computer. "Enter cab" or simply "Enter" is sufficient.

Usually it's acceptable if your sentences contain a verb and an object. There are a few instances in which you will have to use a second object, such as "Sharpen knife with stone". Simply entering "Sharpen knife" wouldn't work because the program needs to know what will be used to sharpen it.

Gametips

The Vocabulary

Although Larry's grammar is simple, his vocabulary is anything but simple. We've compiled a list of the most important words. While we can't explain everything that happens in Larry's adventures, we do know that this is the vocabulary you'll need to master for all three Larry games.

To discourage children from playing the Larry games, the player has to answer a series of questions before beginning play. These tests are designed to keep young players from playing the game. Sierra On-Line intends the Leisure Suit Larry series to be humorous, harmless endeavors for adults only. Parents should carefully consider whether these games should be played by children.

Since Leisure Suit Larry is played worldwide, international players unfamiliar with American slang or personalities may have a difficult time answering the "test" questions. The following list includes explanations of the terminology for the reference of international players only.

The number or numbers following each word indicate the Larry game most likely to contain the word.

Agnew,1	Spiro, former American vice president.
Airsick,2	Refined term for an unrefined condition.
Alaska,1	Largest state in the U.S.A.
Allen,3	Woody, a.k.a. Allan Steward Konigsberg, actor, author, director and clarinet player. Shot all kinds of films, but not "Interiors".
American Pie,1	Song by Don McLean, about a dead rock star.
Analgesic,3	Pain-killer
Andy Griffith Show,3	Not an off-shoot of another program.
Animal Husbandry,3	Mating of animals. Necessary for breeding livestock.

The Larry Story

Answer,1	1. noun
	2. verb
Apple,1	What Eve ate.
Arms control,3	Limiting the development of arms.
Ashes,2	Dust or remains of anything that is burnt.
Ashtray,1	Container for cigarette ashes. Unfortunately, it is also used as a garbage can.
Ask, 1,3	1. to ask for something
	2. to ask someone to do something, to request
At, 1,3	Preposition
Away, 2	As in "to throw something away".
Baby Boom, 3	Increase in the birth rate after World War II.
Back,1	1. preposition
	2. noun
Bag, 2	You can put all kinds of things in here.
Bakker, 1	Jim, former TV evangelist. Not a Larry player's favorite star.
Bangles, 3	Not a 60's rock group.
Bar, 1,3	One of Larry's favorite hangouts.
Bar Mitzvah, 3	Jewish religious ceremony, celebrates a boy's becoming a man.
Beatles, 1	Rock group. One of their more popular songs was "Let It Be".
Bed, 1	You can do all kinds of things on one of these. Larry would like to, too.
Belushi, 1	John. Actor who appeared in "Saturday Night Live".

Bench, 3	You sit on it.
Bench press, 3	Body building device, a kind of thumb screw in health clubs.
Big Bang, 3	Theory on how the universe began.
Bikini, 2	Two piece women's bathing suit. Men look a little funny in one.
Binoculars, 3	Part of every voyeur's equipment.
Blackjack, 1	Card game with a high amount of risk for a lot of money. Also called 21.
Blow, 1	You can blow up a rubber duck or blow out a candle. There are other meanings for which you can use this verb.
Board of Ed.,3	The Topeka Board of Education vs. Brown trial was about desegregation.
Borscht belt, 3	Popular area for comedians.
Boss, 1	Responsible for handing out paychecks on time.
Bottle, 1,2,3	You can put all kinds of things in one of these: water, wine, hair restorer or pills.
Bra, 3	You can put all kinds of things here.
Brain four, 3	Helps you think.
Brando	Marlon, actor
Branch, 2	1. part of tree
	2. part of a company
Breath, 2	Doesn't cost anything (take a breath). Important, especially after you've been holding your breath for a while.
Breath spray, 1,2,3	You can also use it if you don't feel like brushing your teeth.

The Larry Story ——————

Browner, 1	Herbert, former US Attorney General.
Bush, 2	1. American president. Still hasn't turned up in Larry's adventures.
	2. Shrub
Button, 1,3	You can find one on a jacket or on a machine. In the second case, it's a good idea to press it.
Buy, 1,2	To acquire possessions. You don't always need a bill of sale to do this.
Cab, 1	Taxi
Caine, 1	Kwi-Chang, main character of a television show. Originated the saying: "Aaaaaiiiigeeeeaagggh".
Call,1	Verb. You can call all kinds of things. Taxis, dirty names, people.
Canada, 1	Northern neighbor country of the United States. Canadians live there.
Canasta, 3	Card game.
Candy, 1	Dentists love it just as much as ladies do.
Canyon, 3	It's easier to fall into one than it is to cross it.
Capt. Kangaroo, 3	He had a bunny rabbit and a talking grandfather clock.
Card, 1,3	As in a card game or card key.
Carve, 3	Verb, To create figures out of wood.
Casino,1,2	Gambling den with style, bars, shows and a hotel. A favorite hangout of Larry's.
Change, 2	Verb. You can change your mind, your money, or your clothes.
Channel, 1	There are channels that lead out to sea, and T.V. channels.

Chapel, 1	Not just for worship. There are also chapels where marriages are performed for cash on an assembly line basis.
Cheerleader, 3	There are too many of them in the United States.
Chinese War, 1	Hasn't started yet. One of the few wars in which the United States wasn't involved.
Clark, 1	John, former U.S. Attorney General.
Clerk, 2	Employee. Could be anyone from a porter to a salesperson in a drugstore.
Climb, 1,3	Although Larry is after the easy life, he's been known to climb through an occasional window or over a balcony railing.
Close, 3	You're supposed to close doors. Otherwise there's a draft.
Clothes, 2	Cover and protect from cold and wind. You can also change them if your white polyester suit is too conspicuous.
Coconut, 3	The only nut in Larry games that you don't have to crack.
Condominium, 3	Fancy name for apartments.
Crawl, 2	Verb. Creeping along on hands and knees.
Credit, 3	Larry doesn't have any of this.
Curl, 3	As in leg curl, an exercise performed in a health club.
Cut, 1,2,3	You need a knife to cut.
Dance, 1,3	Even if Larry is a bit lazy, dancing seems to be his strong point.
Date, 3	You make a date when you want to get to know somebody.

David Copperfield, 3	Novel by Charles Dickens.
Decree, 3	As in a divorce decree.
Deed, 3	Title to real estate.
Deodorant, 3	Fortunately, computers can reproduce sounds and pictures, but not smells. Larry has his own, unique body odor.
Desk, 1	A proper desk is equipped with various buttons that strangers shouldn't push.
Detente, 1	A policy that is supposed to replace war.
Disco, 1	You mean you really don't you know what a disco is?
Dive, 2	Diving under water opens up completely new perspectives.
Divorce, 3	Not in effect until the divorce decree is available.
Doll, 1	There are dolls that are already finished. There are other dolls that you have to finish yourself. For example, you have to blow up rubber dolls.
Dollar, 2	American money. Very welcome in other countries.
Door, 1,2,3	There is hardly a door that Larry doesn't open.
Doonesbury, 1	Michael, comic artist and inventor of the Walden Puddle Commune.
Down, 1,2,3	Preposition. Indicates a direction, as in sit down, climb down.
Dress, 3	Dress, suit. Suitable wardrobe for all participants in a Larry game. (Put on your tie!).

Drink, 3	1. Noun. Something you order in bars; drink and get happy.
	2. Verb. What you do to get a drink into your body. It's easy: Open mouth, pour beer in, close mouth, swallow.
East Coast, 1	Place in the United States where people talk funny.
Edsel, 1	Not a very successful car.
Eisenhower, 1	Dwight D. 34th president of the United States, 1953-61, nickname "Ike".
Elvis, 1	Presley. Singer of corny, sentimental songs. Not responsible for "What'd I say".
Enter, 1,2	You can enter rooms, houses, boats and taxis.
Envelope, 3	Can contain the most wonderful surprises: overdue notices, indictments, dismissals.
Fasten, 1	Verb. To connect things together (e.g., paper fastner).
Fennel, 1	Vegetable. Its seeds are used as a spice.
Fiji, 1	Group of islands that do not belong to Hawaii.
Fill, 3	You can fill empty bottles, but then they won't be empty any more.
Find, 3	Verb. Locate (e.g., find money)
Flintstone, 1	Fred, cartoon character. Not a Larry player's favorite star.
Floor, 3	Can be used instead of "ground".
Flowers, 2	The most important parts of a flower are the blossoms, that is, the sex organs.
Food, 2	Groceries. What you need to keep from starving.

The Larry Story ——————

Ford, 1	Gerald. 38th president of the United States 1974-1977. Was not elected, but took Nixon's place. He thought he could solve economic problems by wearing a WIN (Whip Inflation Now) button. Other than that, he didn't do anything worth remembering.
Four, 1	What you press in the elevator to get to the fourth floor.
Fruit, 2	You can eat it. It's good for thirst and hunger (except for bananas and coconuts).
F**k, 1	If you really don't know what this word means (clue: it's a verb), you're a lot better off playing "Fish" or "Candyland".
Funicello, 1	Annette, one of the original Mousketeers.
Gestapo, 3	German Secret Police during the Third Reich and World War II.
Get, 1,2,3	If you get tired of saying "take this" and "take that", try "get".
Girl, 1,2,3	The actual reason Larry gets involved in these adventures.
Give, 1,2,3	Verb. Supposedly it is better to give than receive. Careful. The New Testament is limited in its application to Larry, and whatever you give away is often lost forever.
Glass, 3	A glass of whiskey provides unexpected pleasure; a glass with tips in it is sometimes the only way you can get by.
Golfer, 1	Person who dreams of making a "hole in one".
Gone With The Wind, 1	Four hour movie.

Gown, 3	Robe, evening dress. Not exactly the right clothing to wear for an adventure, but you can't always be choosy.
Grass, 3	Grows out of the ground. Softer than concrete.
Hammer, 1	"If I had a hammer...", Old folk song. Great for breaking things.
Handle, 2	Found on suitcases, emergency exits, or windows.
Hard disk, 1	Better than floppy diskettes.
Harness, 2	For horses.
Her, 1,3	Personal pronoun. For example, "Give her anything...".
IBM, 1	International Business Machines. Well known manufacturer of typewriters.
Inch, 3	12 inches is a foot.
Insurance, 2	Insurance salesman aren't the only ones that sell this. Thank God!
Interface protocol, 3	Foreplay between two computers that are united.
Into, 1,2,3	Preposition. You can go into all kinds of things. Even your own downfall.
Jump, 1,2,	Verb. Larry seldom jumps. Only if it's an emergency, or if he can't think of anything else to do.
Kennedy, 1	Ted. Also has two dead brothers. All three were or are politicians. Remembered for his driving style and what he did underwater.
Key card, 3	Plastic card with magnetic media. Frequently used in hotels and health clubs. It's easier to carry and harder to duplicate than an ordinary key.

The Larry Story

Kid, 3	Child, youth. Larry players are not kids.
Kissinger, 1	Henry, United States Secretary of State. Born in Germany.
Klein, 1	Calvin. Famous American fashion designer.
Knife, 1,2,3	No Larry game would be complete without one of these. After all, it's an adventure game, in spite of Larry.
Knock, 1,3	Verb. Knock on wood, for example.
Land, 3	Valuable piece of property, as long as there's no quicksand on it.
Las Vegas, 1	Famous gambler's town, not to be confused with Lost Wages.
Lei, 3	Wreath of flowers - traditional greeting of the South Sea. Natives hope that the tourists are allergic to them.
Lie, 1	Verb. To lie down, for example.
Lifeboat, 2	Who would you want to spend five weeks in a lifeboat with, draw the shortest straw and be eaten?
Light, 2	1. Noun
	2. Verb
Light bulb, 1	Hardware - just don't let a programmer get his hands on one.
Locker, 3	Found in dressing rooms, usually with a picture that's worth looking at twice.
Log, 3	Large chunk of tree.
Look, 1,2,3	Verb. The most important word in Larry's vocabulary.

LSD, 3	Lysergic acid diaththylamide. Capable of creating a considerable amount of disorder in your head.
Lubber, 1	Slang expression for prophylactic.
MacAuliffe, 3	General. Hero of the "Battle of the Bulge".
Macintosh, 1	1. type of apple
	2. Apple computer
	3. Raincoat
Magazine, 1	Can be purchased in many liquor stores. Can contain fascinating articles.
Magic marker, 3	Wide felt-tip marker.
Mailbox, 3	The place where the mailman drops all kinds of things.
Maitre, 2,3	Maitre d'Hotel. Extremely gifted conversationalists. Wants only one thing: A tip.
Make, 3	To create, manufacture. For example, a person skilled in handicrafts can make leis or grass skirts.
Man, 1,2,3	Men appear in all of Larry's adventures. Sometimes it's a good idea to talk to them.
Mansfield, 1	Jayne. Certainly not a sportswriter.
Marijuana, 3	Cannabis sativa, from hemp. Does strange things to your head. Never been out of style.
Marry, 1	Leads to marriage. Practice differs from culture to culture. Sometimes there are strange rites, such as in Lost Wages. The results can be even stranger than the rites.
Marx Brothers, 3	Actors and comedians. The five original Marx brothers were, Groucho, Chico, Harpo, Gummo and Zeppo.

The Larry Story

Mason-Dixon Line, 3	Surveying boundary.
Masters & Johnson, 3	Well known researchers in the field of sexuality.
Matches, 2	Larry doesn't smoke, but occasionally he needs matches.
McCartney, 3	Paul. Singer. Formerly with the Beatles, then with the Wings, then with Linda.
McGraw, 3	Ali, actress. She died in "Love Story".
Mirror, 3	When you look into one of these, you see your reflection.
Mitchell, 1	John, former U.S. Attorney General.
Mohammed Ali, 3	Boxer, real name: Cassius Clay. Remembered for many skills.
Molecule, 1	Rather small. In one glass of water, there are more molecules than there are water glasses in the entire world.
Money, 1	Larry needs this to go shopping, get married and ride taxis.
Monopoly, 1	Game in which you need to own four houses before you can build a hotel.
Mork, 1	Television character from outer space. Comes from the planet Ork.
Move, 3	You move an object from one place to another.
Naked lunch, 3	Novel by William S. Borroughs. Cult book of the beatniks.
Nightstand, 2	Favorite storage place for all kinds of things.

Nixon, 1,3	Richard, 37th president of the United States 1969-1974. Forced to resign because of the "Watergate Scandal", made famous by his appearance in "Laugh In".
NORML, 1	Citizen's initiative that lobbies for the legalization of marijuana.
Oil glut, 3	Oversupply of oil on the world market.
Off, 3	As in "to turn off".
Offer, 3	To achieve his goal, Larry will make the strangest offers.
On, 1,3	Active as in "switched on", atop, and "jumped on"
Open, 1,2,3	You can open anything that is closed. Especially doors, nightstands, lockers, emergency exits and windows.
Orchids, 3	Flowers that boys use to make wreaths.
Order, 1	Larry is not the type to order something out of a catalogue, except maybe a suit. It's more likely he will order everything at the bar: beer, wine, whiskey. That's about all he can think of and all he can hold.
Oswald, 1	Lee Harvey. Assassinated John F. Kennedy.
Out, 1,2	Climb out, lean out, work out.
Over, 1,3	To jump over the fence, for example.
Palm, 3	You won't be able to get Larry on a palm tree. You will see a young lady harvesting coconuts there.
Pamphlet, 2	Leaflet to convince somebody you don't know of something he's never heard before.

The Larry Story

Panama Canal, 1	Linked the Atlantic and Pacific oceans.
Panty, 3	What women wear instead of long underwear.
Pantyhose, 3	Most visible part of women's underwear.
Parachute, 2	Sometimes the best guarantee for a safe landing.
Pass, 1	ID, membership card. Entitles bearer to visit private clubs, where Larry's got no business being.
Passport, 2	Entitles bearer to enter planes, ships and foreign countries.
Pauling, 3	Linus, never received the Nobel Prize.
Pay, 1,2	Verb. If you forget to do this, you might end up dead.
Penthouse, 1,3	Top floor of many hotels: Bungalow on the roof with a garden.
Pesticide, 3	Kills insects.
Peter Piper,1	Picked a Pile of Pickled Peppers.
Philanthropist, 3	Humanitarian
Philatelist, 3	Stamp collector
Phone, 1	Invented by Alexander Graham Bell (1876). Archaic form of data transmission.
Pick, 2,3,	You can pick flowers, apples, your nose...
Pig, 3	On Nontoonyt there are two kinds of pigs: the tame ones are called wild boars and the untamed ones are in houses. Both kinds are dangerous.
Pills, 1	In Lost Wages there are different kinds of pills. Some of them do strange things to your head, others will kill you immediately.

Pin, 2	Sometimes you find one of these in your food. Careful: don't swallow it.
Pink Floyd, 1	Rock group. Recorded "Dark Side of the Moon" in 1973. Highly recommended.
Plaque, 3	Made of bronze, records heroic deeds for all time.
Platform shoes, 1	Shoes with high heels. Probably the shabbiest fad of the 70's.
Play, 1	Verb. Main occupation of most people in Lost Wages.
Politicians, 1	They all live on public funds.
Pot, 3	Slang expression for marijuana.
Press, 3	For example, newspaper, pressed juice, bench press.
Puberty, 1	You are already out of puberty when you play Larry games.
Pull, 3	As in bar pull in a health club.
Push, 1,3	As in push a button.
Put, 2,3	Favorite verb of the English language, if you can't think of a verb, try put. It usually works.
Quayle, 3	Danforth, vice president of United States in 1988. Was not a second Jack Kennedy. Never ready on time.
Radio, 1	Television without the picture screen.
Railing, 1	Supposed to prevent people from falling down. Doesn't do a thing for Larry.
Read, 1,3	Verb. What you are doing right now (no, not with your finger in your nose, with your eyes on the page).

The Larry Story

Remote Control, 1	Nowadays you can't watch television without one of these. Enables you to switch from program to program without getting up from the couch.
Reagan, 1,3	Ronald. 40th president of the United States 1981-1989. Was the main character in "Bedtime for Bonzo" but never a professional football player.
Remove, 1,3	You can remove your clothes (Larry's favorite) or a dictator from office. The same word, just a different action.
Ring, 1	The flower children of the 60's knew that "Love is a ring that has no end". Larry has no use for such nonsense.
Rip, 3	Verb. There are even women who will rip off their own clothes.
Roberts, 1	Oral, Television evangelist. Has his own university but some believe he fell off his rocker a long time ago.
Rock, 3	Stone, boulder.
Rolling Stones, 1	Rock group. Produced an album in the form of a pair of blue jeans - including a zipper that worked.
Rope, 1,3	You can't have an adventure without a rope. That's just the way it is.
Rose, 1	Larry sometimes carries a bunch of these around.
Round, 1	Around.
Sergeant Pepper, 1	Leader of the Lonely Hearts Club Band.
Sewing kit, 2	Contains needle and thread, hammer and sickle. Things that you need.

Sex, 1	A wonderful thing.
Sinatra, 1	Frank. Crooned romantic, sentimental songs.
Shadow, 1	Comic book hero who knows "what evil lurks in the hearts of men".
Sharpen, 3	To make something sharp that was blunt.
Shop, 1	Preferably a liquor shop where you can also buy other stuff.
Show, 1,2,3	1. Verb, to display 2. Noun, Performance
Sink, 1	Wash basin. You find the strangest things in sink drains. Not always a pretty sight.
Sit, 1,2,3	Verb. You can eat, drink, talk and wait more comfortably while you are doing this.
Skirt, 3	Traditional male trousers in the southern hemisphere of this planet.
Slot machine, 1	If you put one of these in the right spot in Lost Wages, it's better than robbing a bank when you need money.
Smash, 1	Verb. Careful, if you smash a pane of glass with your bare hands, you might get an infection.
Soap, 2,3	Do I really need to explain what this is for?
Social Security, 3	A kind of government business.
Soda, 2	Good for thirst, but doesn't make you happy.
Speed, 3	The highest speed you can attain when you jump from a 40 story building doesn't really matter.
Spinach, 2	Makes sailors and little children stronger. Contains a lot less iron than they used to think.
Spirochete, 1	Virus that causes syphilis.

The Larry Story

Spouse, 1	Don't give him/her herpes.
Stairs, 3	Ingenious means of conquering heights without flying.
Stevens, 3	Cat. Religious singer/songwriter.
Stick, 2	Valuable for beating someone, for example to chase them away.
Streaking, 1	Term used in the 70's for running around naked.
Suit, 2,3	Larry's suit is white and made of indestructible, sweat producing synthetics.
Suitcase, 2	Big rectangular bag, that is only interesting after you open it up.
Sunscreen, 2	Suntan oil. Never lie in the sun without it. Your skin is a lot more sensitive than you think.
Sweats, 3	Jogging suit. The worst thing you can wear in public.
Swim, 2	The only sensible activity when you are out on the high seas and you discover that you left your ship at home.
Swimsuit, 2	Sinfully expensive article of clothing worn to prevent you from looking sinful.
Switch, 1,2	1. Verb. What you have to do to start a machine.
	2. Noun. Button or lever you press to start a machine.
Take, 1,2,3	The second most important word in Larry's vocabulary. Larry can take almost anything, except advice.
Talk, 1,2,3	The fourth most important word in Larry's vocabulary. Why worry about what Larry should say? Just give him the command "talk to ..." and he'll think of something. Sometimes.

Taxes, 1	Ought to be abolished.
Taylor, 1	Elizabeth, actress.
The, 3	Definite article. You don't have to use it to be understood by the program.
Thespian, 3	Actor with outdated opinions.
Through, 1,2	Preposition. Through thick and thin, etc.
Throw, 2,3,	Verb. Sometimes it is useful to throw something away - even food.
Ticket, 2,3	For planes, ships, admission.
Tie, 1,3	Verb. You can't have an adventure without a rope, but you have to be able to tie it somewhere.
Timer, 2	A practical device. Press a button and nothing happens. Five minutes later, it's all over.
Tire iron, 3	Expression without any kind of double meaning.
Tip, 3	What you get when you serve the public.
To, 1,2,3	Universally used preposition. Used to express the direction an action should go in, as in "talk to the girl".
Top, 2,3	1. Noun. Half of a bikini.
	2. On top. Depends on the description.
Towel, 3	The more you use it, the wetter it gets.
Trash, 2	A window washer falls into the trash. Two children walk by and say, "Gosh, just look at all the stuff adults throw away". Already heard that one? Never mind. Pay attention to what is thrown away in Larry games.
Tree, 3	You can run into it or climb it, depending on your personal preference.

The Larry Story

Trilateral Comm., 3	International commission engaged in exchanging currency.
Tub, 1	Jump in and have a ball.
Turn, 1,2,3	1. Verb. An activity that allows you to see the other side of the coin.
	2. Verb. To switch, as in "to switch on the radio".
TV, 1	Radio with pictures, movie theaters minus the popcorn. In the "personals" section of the want ads, it can also mean Transvestite.
UNCLE,3	Abbreviation for United Network Command for Law Enforcement.
Under, 2	Preposition. If you want to go over something, under is the other direction.
Undress, 1	Verb. Doesn't happen as often as you may think. Larry just isn't that kind of a guy.
Unplug, 3	Remove a plug from an outlet.
Untie, 1	The only way to remove a rope without cutting.
Up, 1,2,3	Preposition, as in "throw up".
Use, 1,2,3	The third most important word in Larry's vocabulary. If you don't know what else to do with an object, "use" almost always helps.
Utah, 1	State where Catholics, Jews and fresh water are in short supply.
Vertigo, 3	1. Film by Alfred Hitchcock.
	2. Sense of dizziness.
Vine, 2	Tarzan swings to and fro and fro and to on one of these.
Virgins, 1	The best place to look for them is at St. Mary's Girls School.

W-4, 3	Tax form.
Waist, 1	Some people have convex waists, some have concave waists. The latter are easier to tie up.
Walk, 3	Verb, used in "walking the dog". One of the few phrases that doesn't have a double meaning.
Wall, 1	Sometimes you stare at the wall and get an idea. Sometimes.
Water, 3	"I don't drink water - fish f**k in it" W.C. Fields.
Watergate, 1,3	1. Hotel where the Republicans spied on the Democrats.
	2. Scandal that forced Richard Nixon to resign.
Wear, 2,3	Verb, as in to wear clothing.
Westworld, 1	Science fiction movie about an amusement park where the guests are served and entertained by robots.
Whiskey, 1	American spelling of a drink that is spelled Whisky in Scotland, tastes better there and makes you happy anywhere.
Wig, 2	Symbol of dignity at English courts. Not just used to find out the truth, however.
Window, 1	Holes, in the wall, that you look through; don't try to walk through them.
Wine, 1,3	The man of the world drinks wine.
Wire, 3	Your computer will shut down, if you pull this out of an outlet.

The Larry Story

With, 1,3	Yet another preposition. Actually the only preposition you really need to be understood by Larry. Sometimes it's not enough to tell Larry what to do, you also have to tell him what to do it with.
Wood, 3	We aren't made of wood. We're also not made of cast iron, so be careful.
World, 1	Spherical body.
Wozniak, 1	Steve, co-developer of the first Apple computer.
Zadora, 1	Pia, actress and singer. Not one of a Larry player's favorite stars.

2.   Leisure Suit Larry 1:
The Land of the Lounge Lizards

Our story begins shortly after our hero Larry Laffer's fortieth birthday. Up until recently, he led a secure, boring life of poverty. He was a "bachelor by conviction" (also by lack of opportunity), who lived at home with Mother and spent his evenings at home reading his favorite book ("What you've always wanted to know about the RS232 Interface, but were afraid to ask"), or listening to his Barry Manilow records. His life would have continued like this, quiet and sheltered....until, one day it happened. What happened? There are varying opinions. Larry claims that he had had enough of that life and wanted a change. Other people say that Mother had had enough of him, wanted a change, and threw him out. She then took off for Florida, without leaving a forwarding address.

Whatever the case may be, "it" had happened, and Larry bravely tried to make the best of it. Guided by his heroes (Barry Manilow, John Denver and Liberace), he changed his appearance. He got his hair "styled" at the barber shop and bought a suit at the "Night Fever Polyester Plaza Boutique" that turned Larry Laffer into "Leisure Suit Larry": a white polyester suit with open collar, gold chains all over the place. Irresistible.

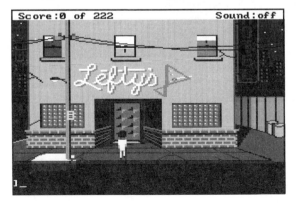

After changing his appearance and personality, he was ready to plunge into the night life. After one or two tries in his home territory (Ball of the Lonely Hearts), he felt he was ready for the big time: a night in Lost Wages, city of night clubs.

45

The Larry Story

We meet our hero shortly after his arrival in Lost Wages. Just arrived, he stands on the sidewalk, undecided. He looks at the sign, "Lefty's Bar". Not very promising, but good enough to start the night. He opens the door and walks into the bar.

The bar looks as promising on the inside as it did on the outside: Not at all. However, this doesn't matter. He finds a spot at the counter, listens briefly to his neighbors' conversations, decides not to bother with them, and orders a beer. It costs him three dollars. The beer leaves him feeling slightly dizzy. Then he tries whiskey.
1 point

Holding a glass of whiskey in his hand reminds him of old Humphrey Bogart movies. So Larry decides that, instead of guzzling it down like a man, it would

be more "macho" to walk through the bar holding the glass of whiskey in his hand. While walking through the bar, nature calls and he looks for the bathroom. The hallway to the bathroom is even more run-down than the bar and Larry becomes more apprehensive. He gathers his courage and addresses the drunk sitting on the floor. After a short chat, Larry feels benevolent and gives the man his whiskey. He doesn't get the shirt off the drunk's back, but he does get the last valuable the old drunk owns. Touching, isn't it?
3 points

While Larry is all choked up, he fumbles blindly on a table in the hall and takes what he can get.
4 points

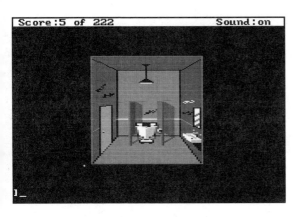

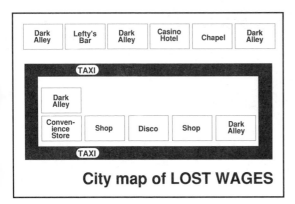

Nature begins to call louder and louder, and he timidly enters the toilet. As he relieves himself, he studies the graffiti on the wall. Some interesting things are written there.
5 points

"Wash your hands after every meal and before you use the bathroom". Or something like that; anyway Larry washes his hands.

While he is washing, the sink catches his eye. It's unbelievable what some people leave lying around places like this. Larry takes what he can get, leaving guilty consciences to other people.
8 points

Larry doesn't stay in the bar much longer. After all, he didn't come to Lost Wages to get drunk, but to indulge in other vices. He leaves the bar and looks around.

Since the area doesn't inspire his confidence, he calls a taxi instead of walking.

The taxi driver lists off the sights of the city. There is a disco full of chicks, a casino right next to a wedding chapel with

round the clock service, and a convenience store that is open all night. Since the taxi driver highly recommends the convenience store Larry has him drive to the store so he can complete his Saturday Night outfit.
9 points

Before Larry is completely out of the taxi, he bumps his head on a pole containing a public telephone. However, he has decided to go shopping. Larry inspects the store and sees: shelves with magazines, beverages, and a small, handwritten sign advertising condoms. Larry doesn't want to miss anything, so he buys everything.
15 points

In front of the convenience store Larry becomes interested in the telephone. In his favorite book about the RS232 Interface there was a chapter that mentioned this gadget. He has to try it out.

On the telephone there are even some numbers that he can use to test out the telephone.
16 points

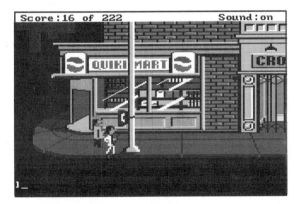

(By now, Larry could be having some trouble with his breath. This becomes apparent when he gets a taste in his mouth that reminds him of a gas station attendant's glove. Oh well, nothing a little breath spray can't handle.)

Before he gets any farther, another drunk starts talking to him. After a short conversation, Larry finds his heart again and gives the poor man a drink. Once again there is a reward for his good deed; the drunk gives Larry his last valuable, which Larry takes without any remorse.
21 points

Telephone number: 555 - 6969
Even though the telephone test is somewhat disappointing, Larry is fascinated with this new technology. To get some more practice, he calls a taxi and heads for Lefty's Bar.
23 points

After he gets there, he notices the heavy wooden door to the right of the entrance. He has to find out what's behind that door. Without paying attention to the other guests (who are also not paying any attention to him), he knocks on the door, loud and clear. To his surprise, a voice asks him the password.

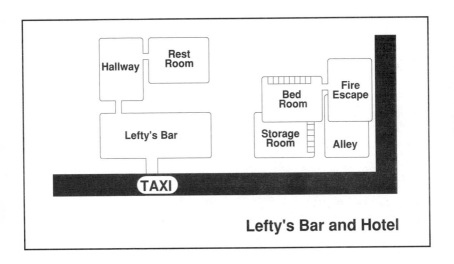

Lefty's Bar and Hotel

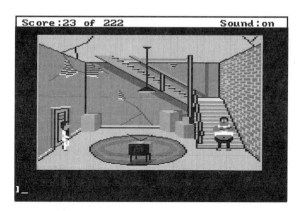

After a while Larry remembers the password and the door opens. But getting in is only half the battle. There is a big bruiser asking for more money than Larry can afford to spend. Maybe he can divert the big ape's attention.

There must be a reason for the television in the backroom. Larry tries to turn it on, but has a hard time. The knob falls off. This is almost as bad as a channel selector that breaks when the televison is tuned to an all sports channel. But Larry has come prepared and knows what to do.
26 points

The television set is on. After changing the channels a few times, Larry manages to find a channel that is on the pimp's wavelength. This enables Larry to go upstairs.
34 points

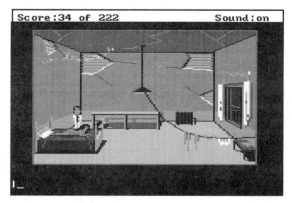

Even though Larry thought the bar bathroom was run-down, it gets even worse: The room above the back room defies description. However, it does have one attraction: A woman.

Larry can hardly control himself. He takes off his clothes. At the last minute, he takes the necessary precaution, jumps into bed and goes to it.
44 points

Ah well. Larry had sex, but it wasn't that great. Somehow it was different than he had imagined. Perhaps he can still find fulfillment. He vows to continue his search for true love. But first, he'd better make himself presentable.
55 points

Before he leaves the scene of the crime, he takes another good look around and takes something no other man has - as a souvenir. Since Larry is always ready for new experiences, he exits through the window and uses the fire escape.
58 points

Of course, he trips. Fortunately he lands in the garbage, so he doesn't get hurt. As long as he's there, he decides to look around and take what he can get before leaving. Then he calls a taxi.
61 points

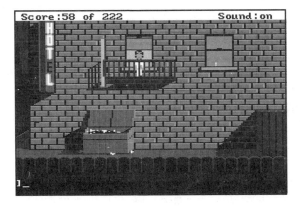

This time he decides to go to the casino. After all, Lost Wages is a gambler's paradise, and Larry has the feeling that he will find true love in the casino.

The Larry Story

In the casino he stands around, undecided. Blackjack or slot machine. Those are the kind of decisions that can keep a guy awake all night.

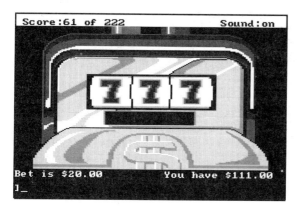

(No matter what you decide, you should fill Larry's pockets with cash. The casino has a limit of 250 dollars, and you should win it all.)

(Don't forget to save on a regular basis because you might lose money, and Larry would be in an awful fix without money.) After winning enough money for the next couple of hours, Larry looks around the casino. Since he is very thorough, he even looks in the ashtray. Of course, he takes what he can get.
62 points

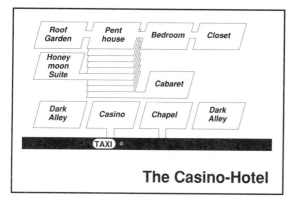

The Casino-Hotel

The show is not as classy as one might expect to find in Lost Wages. Larry is a little disappointed and leaves the casino to try out the disco. In front of the casino Larry meets a man who wasn't as lucky as Larry. As we mentioned earlier, underneath Larry's polyester covered breast beats a heart of gold. Larry helps the poor guy and is once again richly rewarded.
65 points

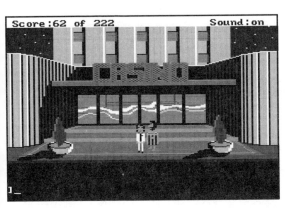

(By the way, you might not meet this unlucky fellow immediately. Have some patience and don't get nervous. At some time in the game he will approach you. Remember, you have a heart of gold.)

The disco is another one of those private clubs. But Larry knows what to do and manages to get in. And, believe it or not, there really is a wild party going on upstairs. Larry has always dreamed of a party like this. Eight characters in white polyester suits are all staring at a lonely blonde. I can do that too, thinks Larry and jumps right in.
71 points

The only empty seat is at the blonde's table, so Larry is obliged to start a conversation with her.

He looks deeply into her blue eyes and talks nonsense. The lady responds accordingly.

Finally, Larry gets a great idea. He'll ask the young lady to dance.
72 points

53

Strange. Larry does know how to dance, even if he can't do anything else.
77 points

After they dance, Larry tries some more conversation. He's about as successful as the last time, until Fawn (the girl's name) winks her eye and asks for money. Larry searches his pockets and gives her what he thinks is appropriate; which is plenty.
92 points

The presents, which Larry gives to her make the right impression. She falls in love with Larry and wants to marry him right away. But in order to do that she needs money. After all, she wants to rent the honeymoon suite in the casino. Larry is generous, gives her the money and promises to meet her at the little wedding chapel next to the casino.
99 points

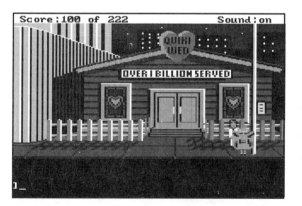

Of course Larry takes a taxi to the chapel. In front of the chapel there is an old man, who is enjoying his hobby. To calm his nerves, Larry jokes around with the man before he enters the chapel.
100 points

In the chapel, Fawn and the justice of the peace are already waiting for Larry. Larry plunges into the adventure and marries Fawn without a second thought. The ceremony is simple. Nobody throws rice, there aren't any flowers, but the justice of the peace insists on drinking to the couple's health. (Over and over again.) Anyway, Larry and Fawn are now man and wife, and as such, ready for

their wedding night. Fawn can't wait any longer and dashes into the casino, and up to the honeymoon suite. Larry has trouble following her.
112 points

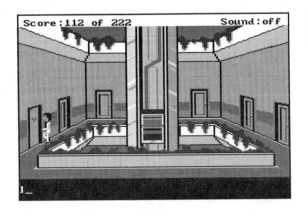

He quickly finds the honeymoon suite in the casino: It's the only door in the entire casino with a heart on it. Larry gets up his courage and enters. The room has everything you could want for a wedding night. A heart-shaped bed, soft lights, atmosphere and a radio, that Larry switches on. After all, you must have music, even if it is sometimes interrupted with commercials.
113 points

Unfortunately, Fawn doesn't have everything she needs to get into the right mood. She would like some wine (a reasonable request). Larry tries to reach room service, but cannot because there's no telephone in the room. He'll have to go somewhere else to make his call.

Fortunately, there is a telephone in the basement next to the elevator. Unfortunately, it's out of order. So Larry has to take a taxi to the nearest telephone. The nearest telephone just so happens to be right in front of the convenience store.

(If you think that Larry could buy his wine at the convenience store and take it back to the hotel: Save your score and try it out.)

The Larry Story

Before Larry can call the Ajax Liquor Store to order wine, the telephone rings and he has to answer it. Another obscene phone call. So what. Larry dials the number of the Ajax Liquor store and orders a bottle of wine for the honeymoon suite of the casino.
123 points

Ajax Liquor Store: 555 - 8039
Since the Ajax Liquor store delivers faster than the speed of light, the wine arrives in the hotel room before Larry does. In the meantime, Fawn has been talking to the delivery boy. After the delivery boy is gone, Larry pours two glasses of wine. Fawn must really need to get in the mood, because she drains the glass in one gulp. Larry fills her glass again and she drains the second.

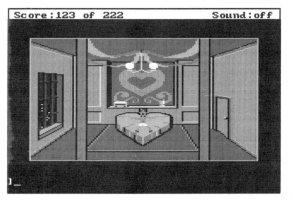

Larry becomes optimistic: This is working.

He kisses Fawn, takes off his clothes, gets into bed and closes his eyes. Now it's Fawn's turn. Unfortunately, Fawn has different ideas about the wedding than Larry. Larry winds up tied to the bed in his underwear. Fawn doesn't just take his illusions, she also takes his money. Fortunately, Larry isn't entirely helpless. After he cuts the rope and puts it in his pocket, he returns to reality, with a bitter heart. To take his mind off Fawn and to get more money, he goes down to the casino and gambles a bit.
136 points

After he has recovered from his shock, he leaves the casino to have a drink. What better place to do that than at Lefty's Bar. While drinking his beer, Larry thinks about what happened to him and wonders whether he made a mistake. But he didn't. Then he realizes that he has forgotten an inconspicuous object that he saw on a windowsill. Larry gets up, knocks on the door to the right of the entrance of the bar and walks past the pimp, up the stairs, past the girl and climbs onto the fire escape. Having arrived, he leafs through his magazine. Then he remembers how to get to the next window where the mysterious object is located.

137 points

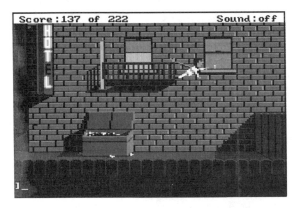

Larry climbs over the railing and gets to the window.

Unfortunately he has to use vandalism, so he breaks the window to get to the object. It turns out to be a pill bottle. "Who knows what this is good for?" thinks Larry and puts the pills in his pocket. Maybe he'll have a headache, which wouldn't be a surprise considering his lifestyle. He climbs back and leaves the fire escape by the shortest route possible.

145 points

Now what should he do with the rest of the night? He doesn't want to go back to the bar, he already bought everything at the store, and the disco also sounds boring. The casino is the only place he still hasn't explored. Maybe he'll find fulfillment there.

After a short trip on the elevator, Larry discovers a floor that is different from the other ones. A receptionist is sitting behind a desk and seems to have been waiting for him. He talks to her. After a short chat, Larry realizes what

stimulants Faith, the receptionist, and he gives her some. The result is overwhelming. Larry has every reason to be jealous of Faith's friends.
150 points

After Faith has cleaned up the scene of the action, Larry has a closer look at the desk. He continues gambling and finds a doorway that has been closed until now. It leads him to the penthouse of the hotel.
155 points

In the penthouse, Larry first goes to the bedroom. There he opens the nearest door and finds himself in the closet again, surrounded by uninteresting junk and an inflatable rubber doll. This seems to be Larry's destiny and he embraces it. He blows the doll up and after hesitating a little, dives on top of

her. Now everything happens like a movie: The doll tears and fizzles out like a balloon. Larry runs after it without thinking and suddenly finds himself in a garden.
173 points

In front of him is a whirlpool, which contains a wonderful woman, named Eve, who doesn't object to the idea of Larry joining her in the whirlpool. Surely this is a dream. The lady shares her champagne with our hero, but she seems to be

waiting for something. Before the water gets too cold, Larry looks around and learns her name. This makes it obvious to Larry what she is waiting for. Larry gives her what she wants and finds what he has been looking for: fulfillment. 213 points

This is frustrating for you, of course. Here you have been helping Larry the whole time and just when it's getting to the good part, the game ends, and Ken Williams appears to tell you about the next Larry game. There is one more thing for you to do: You finished the game with 213 points, not 222. Start over and find the other nine points. This time without our help.

3. Leisure Suit Larry 2: Looking for Love (in Several Wrong Places)

We meet Larry, some time later, back in Los Angeles. Time has taken its toll on our hero; his hair is receding, and the indestructible white polyester leisure suit now stretches tightly over a beer gut.

This is nothing to worry about, however. You're only as young as you feel. That's what they say anyway. And Larry feels young. He often goes to the disco. The girls he meets in the disco are still making him offers. These days, however, they're usually offering him a chair.

Larry mows the lawn in front of Eve's house. He is lost in thought, which is like a foreign country to Larry. This is where our story begins. Eve returns from shopping in an apparent altered state of consciousness. She looks at Larry, thunderstruck, and asks him who he is and why he is mowing her lawn.

Larry tries to refresh her memory. It works. Eve has a vague recollection of the hero of Lost Wages. Prompted by the memories, she gives him five minutes to pack his things and go. Then she sicks her dog on him. In a state of shock, Larry endures the assault of the dog. However, he doesn't realize that the clouds of disaster are ready to start raining over the tropical paradise of Nontoonyt.

Finally the dog leaves, and Larry stands on the street with nothing but a white polyester suit with empty pockets. Although Eve had told him to take all of his things, she didn't give him her house key. The only part of the house still accessible to Larry is the garage. He looks around and, although there isn't much there, takes what he can get.
3 points

The Larry Story

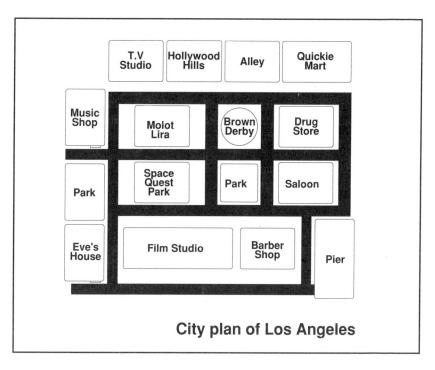

City plan of Los Angeles

Larry wanders aimlessly through the streets of Los Angeles, thinking about what to do. He looks here and there as he walks the streets. Peering behind the

scenes gives him an education on the continuing success of a popular business known to all.
5 points

All the stores are too expensive for Larry. The only exception is a liquor store on the other side of the city.

62

Here he finds a business opportunity that could help him start a new life: He buys a lottery ticket.
8 points

If he's unlucky at love, it's only fair that he should be lucky at games of chance. He has to find out whether his six lucky numbers are winners. To do that, he must go to the television studio that broadcasts the numbers. Larry gets up his courage and enters the studio.

He asks the receptionist if he can win a jackpot with his numbers. Unfortunately, the young lady has lost her glasses and can't make out the numbers on Larry's ticket. She does, however, remember the winning numbers and asks Larry if those are the same numbers on his ticket. After thinking about it, Larry says he has hit the jackpot. Who needs luck when you have no scruples?
18 points

Since they are broadcasting the lottery numbers right now, the receptionist immediately informs the director and asks our lucky hero to wait in the green room. Larry tries to figure out why the room is called the green room when it's not even green. Then a production assistant calls him. Larry follows the young man and arrives in the television studio.
19 points

Somehow Larry had pictured the lottery program somewhat differently. But he accepts his destiny and plays along - what has he got to lose?

After a few moments, it turns out that Larry is the victim of a mix-up; they sent him to

The Larry Story

the wrong show. On this show, three contestants are competing for the favors of bachelorette Barbara Bimbo, an attractive Californian whose hobby is programming computers. Larry has been mistaken for Raguka Singh Soong, a physicist from Pakistan (Ohio), who is one of the three contestants. But Larry doesn't say a word. Barbara is nice looking and Larry has his hopes set on going on a cruise with her.

With more luck than skill, Larry manages to beat the other two contestants, a surfboard waxer and an unemployed journalist. Barbara is furious. She has to spend an entire month on a cruise with Larry. And he doesn't intend to let her get away either.
39 points

Larry receives his prize in the green room and sits down. Before he can catch his breath, a different production assistant takes him to the correct show.
45 points

As the saying goes, unlucky at love, lucky at cards. Larry wins a million dollars, the biggest prize anybody's ever won. That might cover Larry's bad luck in love for the next hundred years or so.
64 points

(From this point on, time becomes critical in Leisure Suit Larry 2. You should save your score often and in different slots. You might end up walking around Los Angeles so long that you miss your cruise.)

What do you do with a million dollars in your pocket? Of course, you go shopping. Larry gets the things he will need for his cruise with Barbara Bimbo.

First of all, he needs his passport. He had to leave it at Eve's house. But perhaps she's changed her mind in the meantime. After all, Larry is rich and famous now. He goes to Eve's house. But she hasn't changed her mind. Even the garage is barricaded. In addition to this, Eve seems to have disposed of all of Larry's possessions. Larry examines the broken pieces of his first relationship and collects what he can still use.

69 points

Now it's time to go shopping. Larry buys a bathing suit and suntan lotion. However, he can't resist the tempting slot machines in the liquor store. Then he goes to the barber shop to get a new hairstyle.

97 points

Some time remains before the ship leaves, so Larry takes a closer look at the only store in the area that has been closed until now, the music store. Of course he starts a conversation with the beautiful Latin American sales girl. Unfortunately, she speaks only Spanish

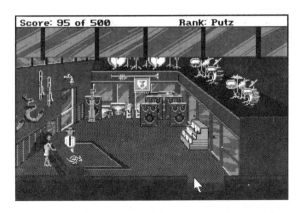

and Larry speaks a rather bizarre version of Spanish. Is it his fault that he had to catch up on his sleep in his high school Spanish class? Or is it his fault that his Spanish sounds like the secret code of the terrible Dr. Nonookee's underground organization? Or is it his fault that it causes him to stumble into a net of espionage and counter espionage that would make Gorky Park look like a Sunday school? (Take time to listen to the dialogue in the music store. It's the funniest dialogue in Leisure Suit Larry 2. Incidentally: As long as there is text on your screen, the clock is stopped so that you can read everything without losing any time.)

Larry leaves the store richer in experience, with an onklunk, the KGB and Dr. Nonookee's agents on his heels.
104 points

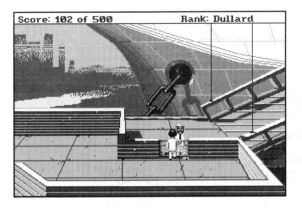

Larry makes it to the ship without any other detours. Now a detour could land him in the KGB's torture chamber. The purser can't help making a few stupid remarks about people who win cruises on game

shows but he lets Larry on board anyway. (Here too, you should save your score as often as you can and store it in different slots.)
113 points

Once aboard, Larry moves into his cabin, which the sailors jokingly call "the last hole". As usual, he takes a look around and picks up whatever he might need.
116 points

After doing his exercises (in hopes of making a better impression on Barbara Bimbo) Larry enters the cabin next to his. There is a lady named Bimbo

waiting for him. However, instead of Barbara, it's her mother. Barbara gave her ticket to her mother, who wants to find a replacement for her deceased husband.

Larry uses the first chance he gets to escape from Mama. Something tells him that it will take all of his strength to survive Mama's attachment to him. He puts on his bathing suit because he wants to go swimming. In spite of this

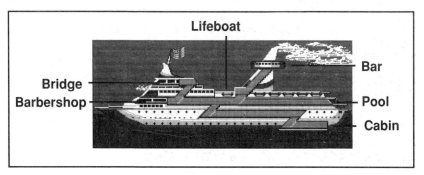

67

noble intention, something holds him back. He enters Mama's cabin one more time and takes what he can get.
122 points

Finally he makes it to the swimming pool. There is an empty lounge chair and Larry lies down to get a suntan. As you know, the rays of the sun are even more intense when they're reflected off the water. The danger of sunburn is much greater too. Of course, these days people protect themselves by applying suntan lotion.
128 points

As expected, a girl comes up and starts talking to him. This doesn't surprise Larry since the bathing suit and hairstyle cost him enough. But Larry doesn't want to play his trump cards too soon, so he cools off with a dip in the pool. At the bottom of the pool he sees a fuzzy object.

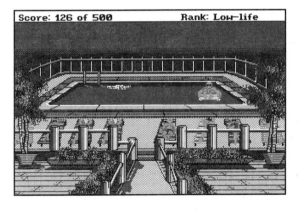

Score: 126 of 500   Rank: Low-life

In keeping with an old tradition, Larry takes what he can get. He takes a deep breath, dives in and gets the object, which turns out to be a bikini top.
135 points

After getting out of the water, Larry remembers that his suntan lotion is no longer effective because it deteriorates in water. He puts on some more lotion and goes back to the cabin to change his clothes. Then he'll explore the rest of the ship.
138 points

The first place he finds is the ship barbershop. Maybe they can do something about his thinning hair. As it turns out, they can. Even though it costs Larry a

Larry 2

lot of money, he's got a lot of hair now. In keeping with an old tradition, Larry then proceeds to the bar and takes...
143 points

His reconnaissance mission leads him to the command deck and the bridge. There his gambler's instinct compels him to push a button. This releases the safety mechanism of the lifeboats. Not a bad deal for Larry, because, in the meantime, he has realized that life on board the ship could become very dangerous for him.
149 points

(We hope you realized in the meantime that several death traps are waiting for Larry. This is more evidence that you should save regularly.)

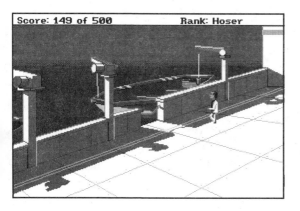

Larry gets the urge to leave the ship as quickly as possible. He heads for the lower deck, where the lifeboats are being automatically lowered into the water. Larry jumps into a lifeboat at the last possible moment.
153 points

Larry doesn't have much time to prepare for his long, uncertain journey in the lifeboat. So much to do in so little time. He has to protect himself against

sunstroke and throw everything that could be hazardous to his health overboard.
165 points

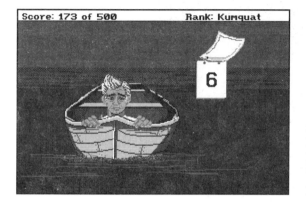

Now he has time to think about his life. Fortunately he has everything he needs: suntan lotion, something to drink, and he can make a fishing pole out of hangers and thread. Fish are healthy to eat because they contain a lot of protein.
190 points

Even the most wonderful sea voyage must eventually end. After ten days and nights in the lifeboat, a storm sweeps him to an uncharted island. (Remember to save as often as possible because Larry is still in danger after the sea voyage.)

Exhausted, Larry sinks into the sand. However, he discovers that civilization has covered this beach with trash. Larry is in a vacation spot. Since KGB agents are guarding the road to the airport, the only thing Larry can do is hide in the jungle.

Larry 2

Surrounded by luxurious tropical vegetation, Larry's sense of beauty awakens and he picks a flower. After wandering around, he discovers a restaurant. Just what the doctor ordered after ten days in a lifeboat. He waits for the hotel maitre'd' to show him to his table. He finds himself surrounded by rich and famous people (Mr. and Mrs. Rich, Mr. and Mrs. Famous and Mr. and Mrs. Gates...). At the buffet his old passion emerges and he takes what he can get.
198 points

After leaving the restaurant, Larry wanders through the jungle again. This time he finds a hotel. Here, too, he takes what he can get.
202 points

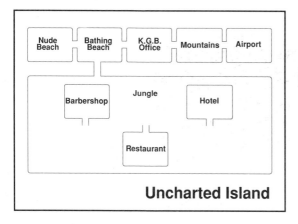

Back to the jungle. This time he wanders into a barbershop and - we've seen this before - gets his hair bleached.
205 points

Larry, in blonde hair, races through the jungle and finds himself back on the beach. The road to the

airport is still blocked. The FKK beach is closed to Larry. Nevertheless, he takes what he can get.
209 points

Larry has no choice but to disguise himself. But where can he change? The only place he can think of is the hotel. To get there he has to go through the jungle, past the restaurant and back into the jungle until he reaches the hotel.

He changes in the hotel and sets off again: through the jungle to the barbershop. Body wax never felt so good.
217 points

On the beach, Larry realizes that his disguise is incomplete; the KGB agents will certainly recognize him the way he looks now. He has to make some more stops. Although he has the necessary objects in his inventory, he needs a place

to change. You already know the way: Jungle - restaurant - jungle - hotel - jungle - barbershop - jungle - beach.
229 points

Completely unrecognizable, Larry finally manages to get

past the KGB agents. The kind words they call out to him don't bother him.
After all, it could have been a lot worse.
241 points

Of course, Larry still has to pass another test before he can be safe. In front of
him is a steep cliff with a small, narrow path as the only passage. Larry is not
only at the mercy of his programmers, who have a macabre sense of humor,
but he also has to find a place to change his clothes, preferably out of sight.
247 points

After a death defying
journey across the
steep cliff, not even
the two KGB Ninja
fighting machines can
keep Larry from
making it to the
airport. Larry says it
with flowers and
enters the airport
terminal.
254 points

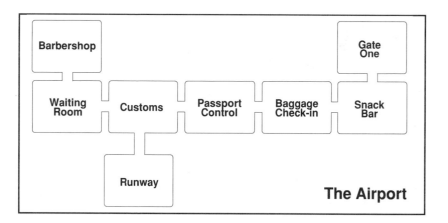

The Airport

(Every second also counts in this phase of Leisure Suit Larry 2. So save, save, save.)

There is another barbershop in the terminal. Are you really surprised that Larry finds it? Well, this time his visit to the barbershop is as disappointing as his last visit was successful. Larry once again looks like the picture on his passport. This doesn't please him. There's a little present for him on top to make up for it.
257 points

Although Larry's face and the picture on his passport now resemble one another, the line at customs doesn't get any smaller. It just doesn't make sense to line up. So Larry, deciding to be rude, cuts in front of everybody else. The customs official cooperates and lets Larry pass after briefly searching him. At the luggage pick-up Larry gets that old familiar feeling. Perhaps there's

something useful in one of the suitcases. He grabs one suitcase after another until he finds something he can use. He becomes a hero, gets to meet the President, is decorated with all kinds of medals, etc. Or maybe not.
282 points

Anyway, now he can buy his ticket. Although time is running out, Larry still takes the time to purchase flight insurance from a vending machine and buys himself a snack. After opening his snack, that either the KGB or Larry's mother prepared for him, he doesn't even have time to eat it. He has to board the plane.
297 points

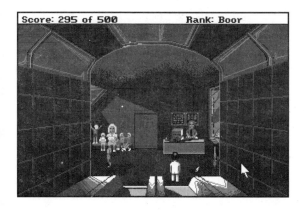

At the check-in counter, out of habit, Larry takes a pamphlet that is lying there and has just enough time to hand his ticket to an airline employee before boarding the plane.
311 points

In the airplane Larry finds all of the modern comforts you would expect. There are friendly stewardesses and plenty of space. In short, everything is as it should be; it's just not for Larry.

Larry takes what he can get while the stewardess is demonstrating safety precautions to the passengers. Then he remembers that the name of the airline looked a lot like "Aeroflot". He'd better get out of here. However, first he must distract the person sitting next to him.
324 points

But how do you leave an airplane that is already in the air? You break the lock on the emergency exit and rely on your flight insurance.
342 points

The Larry Story

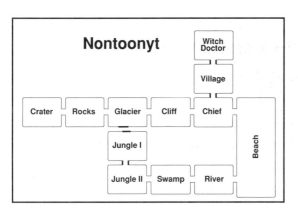

And so, once again, Larry finds himself on a tropical paradise. After freeing himself from the tree, Larry explores the virgin forest.

The onklunk did not survive the hasty exit from the airplane. Larry leaves it in the jungle, along with the secret that several secret service agencies are so eagerly pursuing.
350 points

Instead of the onklunk, Larry takes a heavy stick, which he finds on the ground, with him. You never know how a stick can be used. But first Larry has to find a path around the killer bees. Unimpressed by the prehistoric sculpture, Larry makes his way through the jungle.
360 points

Larry soon finds a use for the stick. It's great for driving off wild animals. But how can he cross the swamp he just stumbled upon? With some quick thinking (and if you save your score in time) he'll easily manage that.
375 points

The only thing between Larry and the beach is the jungle river. Unfortunately, the river is full of piranhas.

Fortunately, Larry remembers stories about an English nobleman who practiced his unusual hobby in light clothing. This also enables him to solve the problem he has crossing the river. Before leaving the jungle, Larry takes what he can get.
385 points

Larry finally reaches the beach. He finds what he didn't dare hope for: a wonderful woman, whom he falls in love with immediately. She also falls in love with him. Our story could end here, except for the fact that you have to earn the love of a beautiful woman.

Kalalau can't go out on a date with Larry because her tribe forbids all forms of prenuptial pleasure. Larry would like nothing better than to marry her. He has

solved all kinds of problems, and besides, he doesn't have anything else planned for the afternoon.

But there's more to the customs of Kalalau's tribe. No marriage can be performed or consummated until the island of Nontoonyt is redeemed from its present curse. That's what the elders decided.

An intruder has seized the natives' sacred burial grounds (the tip of a volcano) and changed them into an impregnable fortress. A true villain, he has hypnotized the most beautiful women of the tribe and is holding them captive in his fortress.

Worst of all, the dreaded Dr. Nonookee has ruined the natives' profitable tourist industry. Now the islanders are waiting for a hero to redeem them from this nightmare.

Larry, of course, has nothing better to do than apply for this job. He is so madly in love with Kalalau that he would not only climb the highest peak of the Himalayan mountains for her but also work out a Desktop Publishing program for her. Kalalau is now in a terrible hurry to introduce Larry to her father, Chief Keneewauwau and the other members of the tribe.

Before they can send him off to free the island from tyranny, Larry must prove that he is worthy of this challenge. The test is cruel and inhuman. Larry has to show that he can master the sacred, mighty tribal totem Peesea, by developing his own program. He can make the program do whatever he wants and it can be as long as he wants. The only requirement is that he write the program in the assembler.

Well, Kalalau is a chieftain's daughter. Larry studies the task for a while and then designs the program EUNUCHS, a multi-user, multi-tasking operating system, that runs on Intel 8088-CPU machines. We won't speculate about why Larry neglects to tell chief Keneewauwau that there already is such a program (named EUMEL, developed at the University of Bielefeld and operated by GMD, St. Augustin by Bonn); after all, he wants to win Kalalau's hand in marriage.

The chief shows Larry the way to the sacred burial grounds, which is the only way to reach Dr. Nonookee. After the chief shows Larry the way, all of the villagers retreat and wait for redemption. Before he leaves, we see that love can indeed have strange effects on people because Larry falls into deep thought. Finally he remembers that Kalalau mentioned a glacier, which Dr. Nonookee uses to cut off access to his fortress. Larry goes back again and takes the necessary precautions.
426 points

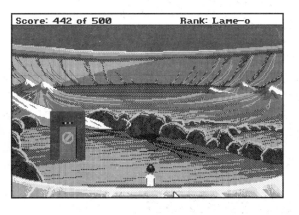

After climbing the glacier and overcoming difficulties that we won't bore you with here, Larry actually reaches the peak of the volcano. However, he is very disappointed. Larry was expecting to find the perverted pleasure garden of Dr. Nonookee, full of beautiful, helpless slave girls. Instead all he finds is an elevator in the crater of the extinct volcano. Needless to say, it doesn't work.
447 points

Disappointed, Larry wants revenge: With his last remaining object from his inventory, he mixes up an explosive and tosses it into the crater, hoping that something will happen.
467 points

Something does happen. The elevator opens up, Larry storms Dr. Nonookee's fortress, frees the hypnotized slave girls, radios for help and takes a helicopter to a happy ending and a last visit to the barbershop.
497 points

Well, that's that. A total of 497 points out of a possible 500, is pretty darn good.
If you're not satisfied with that total, try it again. This time by yourself. Good luck!

4. Leisure Suit Larry 3: Passionate Patti in Pursuit of the Pulsating Pectorals!

The beginning of the third adventure

Fortunately for Larry, he survived the adventure with Dr. Nonookee. Now he spends countless hours of pleasure with his new companion, Kalalau, in love

and, at the moment, out of trouble. Unlike their predecessors, the natives of the island don't allow themselves to be exploited. Instead they control the development of the island themselves.

The Larry Story

They form a monopoly to establish financial security. After a while, Larry develops a certain routine. Thanks to his marriage to Kalalau, Larry is now vice president of Natives Incorporated.

In the first frame of the game, we see a corpulent Larry, dressed in a loud, colorful shirt and watching a girl through binoculars, in memory of the old days when he was a swinger. This gives us a preview of the frames that follow.
2 points

Lost in thought, he examines a commemorative plaque, content with himself and his role on the island. No Leisure Suit Larry player would dream that he was planning to embark on a new adventure. After a few steps in the first frame, you'll move Larry through the untouched, virgin jungle where you're informed of his destination: Kalalau, his beloved companion and spouse, is already waiting for him.
4 points

The virgin jungle of Nontoonyt Island can still provide a few adventures. Larry makes his way to the house he shares with Kalalau. From the driveway he can see her in a hot tub and he yells a greeting. But, unfortunately, Kalalau isn't

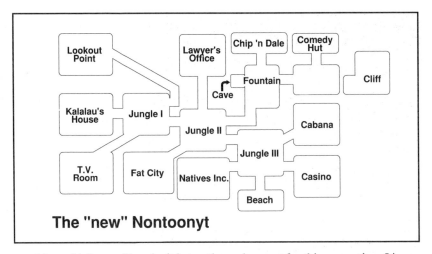

The "new" Nontoonyt

speaking with Larry. You don't know the real reason for this separation. It's also unclear why Larry's companion puts new obstacles in the way of her love.

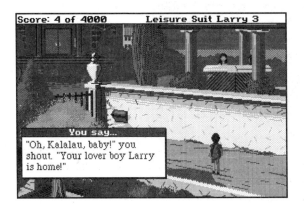

However, Larry is now completely depressed. What should he do now? He wanders aimlessly through the jungle and checks his alternatives: "I could lead a happy-go-lucky life, hang around all day, sit in my room, rent a bunch of videos, things like that...- or I could give up women forever (would this surprise you after everything he's been through?), live a life of celibacy, become a minister or something like that."

Then he pulls himself together: "That's not for me, Larry Laffer. Just think, Larry, this island is the perfect place for an experienced, single playboy like yourself." (One of the many unexpected clues for solving the game follows! Even clues or words that seem unimportant may provide important tips to complete the game. You should either write them down or memorize them.)

"My love for Kalalau probably blinded me to my opportunities on this island. Where could I find more girls than on a tropical vacation resort? And each one of them came for one thing: a good time!" Larry shouts in the silent jungle: "That's it. I've had enough of monogamy, marriage, long lasting relationships and commitments. From now on my new goal will be to let as many girls as possible please me!"

The following scene shows our hero undergoing a transformation, from Larry Laffer (married) to Leisure Suit Larry (single swinger), which is not unlike Clark Kent's transformation to Superman. Now Larry's reborn ... a wearer of an

impressive white polyester suit. After all, white is the color of purity (?) and it lights the way for him.

After deciding to lead a new life, Larry has to think about the material resources he will need in his new life as a playboy.

Until now Kalalau had taken care of him, now he will have to take care of himself. As he walks through the jungle, he thinks about his job as vice president of Natives Incorporated. The president, Kalalau's father, surely wouldn't make life difficult for him, just because he and Kalalau are now divorced. Especially not after Larry had just finished closing a big deal for the company. You'll be unmistakably guided along the same path Larry takes.

Bright neon lights and plastic palm trees line the entrance to Natives Incorporated. In the lobby we see a tiger skin and a row of bottles. The doorman tells Larry that the president (Kalalau's father) wants to see him in his office immediately. He's barely in his former father-in-law's office when he receives this greeting:

"Good morning, Mr. Laffer! It's nice you could find the time to drop in to see me. Won't you sit down?" Since Larry isn't offered the couch, he settles for the zebra skin in the middle of the room.

We can only highlight the scene that follows. The president of Natives Inc. plays a dirty trick on Larry Laffer. Is this because Keneewauwau still doesn't have a Sierra game installed on his Mac computer? Now, not only is Larry out of a job, he also has no pension, medical insurance, severance pay or other benefits. This experience is reason enough to never return to this lobby...

After this, the actual adventure begins. Leisure Suit Larry, broke, without any friends or relationships, sets out to find women that will give him pleasure.

The Larry Story

The first encounter

Larry's complete lack of resources forces him to take desperate measures. The only thing that he has is a copy of the "Nontoonyt Tonite" magazine of cultural events. His only hope is to explore the area and look for useful objects. "Useful objects" is a somewhat vague description. Larry manages by reading his copy of "Nontoonyt Tonite". He finds numerous pointers on local customs, the behavior of the natives, special folklore traditions as well as the latest meeting places, attractions and shows geared for the tourists. In the meantime, you can

occupy yourself with your own copy, which can be found in the game box. For many reasons the magazine is an indispensable tool for Larry's future adventures.

Now the object of the game is to explore different places. Since drawing maps is not much fun, we've inserted various maps of the island and the locations on the island so that you don't have to draw these maps yourself. Keep this in mind: Have Larry look for the Granadilla tree. The wood of this tree is very durable and excellent for carving figures. Sculptures carved out of Granadilla wood are rare and in great demand.
6 points

You should also have Larry return to his former apartment. He'll find an important item in the apartment to add to his inventory. It's unlikely this item was there in the morning when Kalalau was giving him his walking papers.
26 points

Larry 3

Score: 26 of 4000   Leisure Suit Larry 3

Larry's back in the jungle after leaving his former apartment. His walk through the jungle returns him to the place where he decided to lead a swinger's life. There are a total of five passages from this location into other places in the game. Each one is important at a certain stage of the game. With the inventory he has collected so far, Larry's already prepared for the first adventure.

Tawnie's Souvenir

There's no better place to start an adventure with racy women than on the beach. From the square in front of the hotel (there are also five passages to other places here!), Larry proceeds to the dreamlike sand beach of Nontoonyt Island. When he gets there, he sees a beautiful, bare-breasted woman lying on her beach towel obviously enjoying the sun. Before he's able to gain her attention, a souvenir vendor appears peddling his wares loudly and persistently.

The blonde haired beauty, who answers to Tawnie, wakes up and is delighted by the prospect of buying a souvenir without any hassles. Even if it surprises you, pay close attention to Tawnie's compulsive shopping habits. She even listens closely to the sales pitch. (Whoever believes in miracles, finds them on every corner!) Larry will have some trouble with Tawnie's tendencies in this area.

The Larry Story

The souvenir transaction is barely finished when Larry arrives. He gives her an irresistible look and introduces himself, "My name is Larry; Larry Laffer." As she politely stands to talk to him, another souvenir vendor appears to take advantage of the beautiful tourist. Larry ignores the vendor and continues his conversation with her. He stares directly into Tawnie's blue eyes. The conversation quickly drags and prevents Larry from getting closer to his goal of an erotic adventure with this breathtaking beauty. In a mysterious way, Tawnie answers the critical question of what she would need in order to be with an "older man" like Larry, "Larry, I think I'm a very material girl."

Larry has an eye for detail and doesn't always think of his own personal gain. He enables Tawnie to go on a "golden" shopping spree.
48 points

She thanks Larry by giving him a first class erotic ride. But before Larry can get in the mood for this surprising, passionate display of tenderness, another souvenir vendor, who immediately draws Tawnie's attention away from Larry, arrives. Our hero lies defeated on the ground before he could even begin. While he daydreams, Tawnie purchases a knife, at a bargain price, from the vendor.

But Tawnie hasn't forgotten about Larry. The souvenir vendor is barely gone before she turns back to our "single swinger". He's a little hurt by her rude behavior but still cheerful and capable of loving her. Love continues at a furious pace until...

Score: 76 of 4000   Leisure Suit Larry 3

Do you remember how the sand moved when you looked at the beach? Or did you just let Larry look around without noticing this? It's too late now...the beach critters just made themselves at home on him! Larry begins to scream. Tawnie doesn't understand his strange behavior and tells him that he should have known better. She informs him that "I refuse to be with such an irresponsible man! Get out of here you flabby macho jerk!" She no longer speaks with Larry since he doesn't have anything that interests her.
116 points

Now Larry is back where he started. He was in the middle of a promising adventure, tried his best, but gained nothing even though it wasn't his fault. He stands next to Tawnie's beach towel and contemplates his situation. Pressing the tab key lets you know that Larry has already acquired the knife that Tawnie purchased during his attempts at lovemaking. Tawnie isn't concerned with what she buys; she's only interested in buying things. Since there's nothing more for Larry to love here (but perhaps there's something for him to get) he leaves.

Cherri: The big show
Larry strolls aimlessly through the jungle in search of exciting adventures. As he reaches the "Television room", a terrace in the jungle with a television set and a bench, he sees a guide on the table. He sits down on the bench and begins to read the guide. He spots an advertisement for a "girlie show" in the showroom of the hotel. He doesn't find any other promising prospects as he leafs through the guide. Although the television set works, it doesn't show

Larry the pictures he wants to see. Or maybe you're the one chasing Larry through the jungle in search of "lust filled" adventures?

In any case, Larry decides to see the girlie show. Looking at beautiful girls isn't as much fun as flirting with them, but it's better than nothing! The way to the showroom is easy to find. Larry, full of anticipation, rushes in. There are many different ways Larry can enter the hotel, but there's only one showroom.

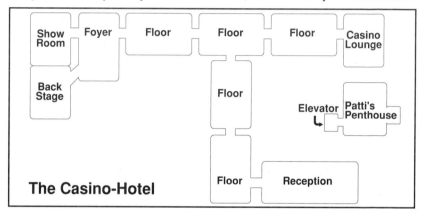

When he tries entering the showroom, Larry meets the doorman. The fierce looking doorman refuses to talk to Larry. Every time Larry tries, he receives a "There is no response" message. Larry gradually realizes that he will have to pay admission.

However, Larry has a copy of "Nontoonyt Tonite" in his pocket. Many of the different hotels and promoters have placed advertisements in this magazine and some include complimentary passes to their shows. Larry shows the doorman his copy containing the tickets. The maitre'de (programmer Al Lowe even knows a few French words!) requests today's ad on a specific page of "Nontoonyt Tonite". Since the page varies according to the day, you'll have to look it up for Larry. Turn to the proper page and read the number on the show pass.

Have Larry repeat the number to the doorman (type them in). Be careful: if you enter the wrong number you'll have to start over from your last saved score. Even if it's the right number, the doorman still won't let Larry in. Rubbing his fingers together, the doorman indicates there is still something missing: Maybe he's practicing karate, broke his hand, or has a nervous twitch. Who knows what else you have to give a doorman in order to get in with a valid ticket.

This doesn't present a problem for a man such as Leisure Suit Larry. Every bouncer opens the door when you grease his palm with some cash. But where is Larry going to get money. Will he have to steal? Your memory will help here. Somebody mentioned having twenty dollars in cash. There aren't that many people in this game!

After sending Larry everywhere, send him back to the person who took all of his money. However, all of Larry's efforts to retrieve the twenty dollars from her fail. All she wants are souvenirs and more souvenirs. Studying "Nontoonyt Tonite" will help because it has some interesting information on the native handicrafts of the island. For example, there is the article about native woodcarvings. Unfortunately the article ends at the most interesting place and continues with the next issue, which you don't have. Just use your imagination: Look at the piece of wood that Larry picked up and imagine yourself in a drunken state. What could you carve out of a piece of wood that women would appreciate? If you still can't think of anything, you're probably one of those people who has to hear a joke over and over before understanding it, especially if it's a dirty joke.

The Larry Story

As an avid player of the Leisure Suit Larry games, however, you've probably already been initiated into the world of dirty jokes. Therefore you know what kind of souvenir to carve. Larry tries to use the wonderful Ginsu® knife. Unfortunately, it takes some effort to get it to work. Larry is unable to use the knife, which he took from Tawnie, right in front of her. Have Larry leave the beach. In the jungle between the hotel and the beach Larry tries to carve the wood again. The knife still doesn't work. Larry looks around and gets an idea on how to get it to work. Now he's made a sharp tool out of the knife, which can now be used for all kinds of work.
166 points

Larry gets down to business and starts carving the Granadilla wood. You'll probably have the same thoughts on what Larry should carve as he does. The level of your play determines how erotic the sculpture becomes after Larry's done carving. Now he must deliver it to Tawnie.

You'll have to try dressing Larry so that he looks like a salesman. No one would buy genuine native handicrafts from a man in a white polyester suit. Or would they?
216 points

Reading the magazine gives Larry another good idea. Along with the "adult" themes, articles on folklore are an important part of the magazine. Anyone who's already seen a movie about Hawaii knows what to do. Larry has already had some experience with the natives (and the business practices of Natives Inc.). All you need to finish Larry's costume is the right kind of grass. Now, where did we see grass? Alright, we'll let Larry look at the card in peace so that he can find the right kind of grass.

After a few tries, you're able to have Larry harvest the grass. Then let Larry finish his disguise. He easily copies the clothing of the souvenir vendor.

Finally, Larry feels like he's getting closer to his goal (remember, he wanted to see the show...)
266 points

All he has to do now is change clothes. Since Larry doesn't want Tawnie to notice, he slips off to a certain place. He disappears and changes clothes. Then he hides his clothes for later use.
276 points

Off to Tawnie! Once he gets there, everything goes as planned. He gets what he needs from Tawnie, who is always on the lookout for a good deal. Then he returns and changes into his regular clothes. At the door, it's business as usual with the doorman, who waits for Larry to explain that he has a copy of "Nontoonyt Tonite" that entitles him to admission. Larry gives the correct ticket number. Then he greases the doorman's palm with a twenty dollar bill. Now nothing stands in his way.

The Larry Story

Cherri's big show

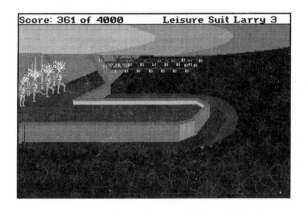

Larry finds a seat in the back and enjoys the girlie show... 361 points

Miss Cherri Tart makes her impressive entrance. Her erotic dance gets the crowd so excited that they toss dollar bills (some shaped as airplanes) on the stage. Larry also is impressed by Miss Cherri Tart. But it's the end of the two hour show - Larry has lost too much time.....

Larry stands in the lobby thinking of a way to meet Cherri Tart. He's extremely confident about his effect on women. Neither talking with the maitre'd or waiting outside the stage door helps. Frustrated, Larry is on the way out when a gorgeous women walks across the stage and turns to the telephone. Larry, here's your chance!

Larry turns on his charm and sweet talks the lady. While others claim he can only talk in one syllable words, Larry maintains, "it's the feeling that counts..." And so they pour their hearts out to each other, the would-be star and the would-be farm girl. After telling each other their goals in life, Larry wants to get closer. As usual, Larry tries to impress her with a generous present. He'll give everything he has to Cherri. She's thrilled.

She makes Larry's mouth water. As soon as he has the necessary documents he should knock softly on her door, where she'll be waiting. Once again, Larry is on the road! 391 points

In case you didn't already know what's going on (since he's been on the island long enough to know about this custom, Larry's already thought of it), you should reacquaint yourself with the traditions of the Nontoonyt island natives. According to custom, Larry has a claim to a part of the land that once belonged to Kalalau. It's one thing to have this claim but quite another to give it as a present. Larry must follow a certain procedure. So Larry begins an adventure within an adventure: He tries to find a lawyer.

Maybe you have already sent Larry to see DeWey, Cheatem & Howe. Until now none of the lawyers have had enough time for Larry's problems. Larry waits for the proper time to approach the young man at the reception desk. All he has to do is submit his request. As he gets up his courage to ask about his legal rights in his separation from Kalalau, he is sent to Miss Cheatem, the attorney.
401 points

The Larry Story

Larry is barely in his chair before the smart lawyer tells Larry how she handles new clients. Despite being energetic and full of purpose, Larry catches only half of what she says. Along with the cost of the divorce, Larry learns about some of the old traditions, such as how they divide up the property. Roger, the secretary of the law firm, is instructed to fill out the necessary papers. This will take a little time, so Larry takes a walk in the jungle. On his way, he decides to take in the comedy show. The legend (in his own mind), Paul Paul delivers another great performance. Nothing like a little ethnic humor to get you through your daily routine. Not really meant for serious people....

431 points

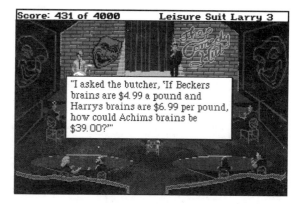

"I asked the butcher, 'If Beckers brains are $4.99 a pound and Harrys brains are $6.99 per pound, how could Achims brains be $39.00?'"

Larry keeps waiting for a good joke as the show drags on. At the end of the show, more exhausted than happy, Larry remarks that the show was better than the one they had several years ago at the Honeymoon Hotel. Then he goes back to the lawyer's

office. He finally gets the deed - made out to the bearer - to 640 acres of rare, untouched woodland. Deed in hand, he heads back to meet Cherri.
551 points

Larry the Star
Full of expectation, Larry knocks on the door to the stage entrance. His hopes are realized: Cherri, overjoyed about her future as a beacon of hope in the rain forest, now fulfills one of Larry's dreams. You'll see Cherri's private show in front of Larry before her next stage performance....

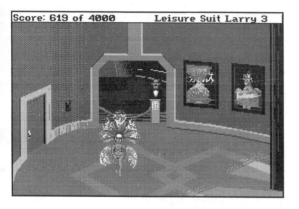

Almost as though expected, a drum roll interrupts Cherri as she plans to fulfill Larry's wish. Cherri shouts, "Get dressed, the second show is beginning." After a lot of hectic running around, the emcee announces Cherri, the lights go on, the curtain goes up and the surprise is there. While Cherri escapes from her role as a sex object, Larry proudly performs his new role.
619 points

Larry accepts the facts concerning his divorce from Kalalau. He remembers the nice lawyer and goes back to her office without changing his outfit. Roger, the secretary, asks Larry if he has brought the money. Without hesitating, Larry pays him. He's allowed to see the lawyer, who's delighted to see him in such a state. Another interruption follows and despite your laughter, Larry's still a frustrated man....

As a result of these experiences, Larry decides to stay dressed in a white skirt. He picks it up and heads for more experiences.

Larry's first advances on Patti

If Larry wants to find out what's happening in Nontoonyt, have him look through the show program again. He'll read:

Now appearing in the Casino Lounge:
Passionate Patti
Keyboard and Sing-A-Long
Star Of Five Continents!
Even Appeared On "Star Search"

Although exhausted from his several failures, Larry becomes curious and heads to the Casino Lounge. There he finds Passionate Patti.

It's not just her name but also his reactions which indicate to Larry that he has finally found the right woman (is that possible with a score of 756 out of a possible 4000 points?). So he strikes up a conversation...

After a few attempts at making conversation, he finally asks Patti for a date. Patti clearly states that enough single men are available. Unfortunately, Larry doesn't have his divorce papers yet. So he has to leave Patti and return to his lawyer's office.

Larry asks Roger for his divorce papers and Roger hands them over. Larry takes a good look at this important document. Oh, what a coincidence, Suzi Cheatem is giving Larry a membership to a health club...
881 points

Back in the Casino Lounge, Larry resumes his conversation with Patti. This time he proudly shows her his divorce papers and makes another attempt to capture her heart. Although her interest in Larry increases, she points out that living on the island has gotten him out of shape. So, he's got a lot to do before he can have his Patti.
981 points

Larry remembers the opportunity Suzi gave him by mistakenly handing him a key with his divorce decree. This would be a good opportunity to get back into shape. So he leaves Patti once again. Before he can go to Fat City, however, he will have to collect some more equipment.

First, Larry has to go to the cabana behind the hotel. If he meets Al Lowe there, he shouldn't start a conversation with him. In the cabana there is a sink. Larry should have a drink here. There is also an important washing utensil that he shouldn't leave hanging here. Anything else he might need for personal hygiene he's already seen during one of his previous adventures with a lady. When he returns to the scene, he can take it with him. (Even 2 points can be crucial to the game!)
997 points

The Larry Story

Fat City

After Larry finally arrives in Fat City, he heads straight for the Aerobic Studio. He's able to open the door thanks to Suzi's help. Bambi, an athletic young woman, is doing aerobics in the studio. As usual, Larry starts a conversation with her. All of his efforts to get her to work off some calories with him fail. His suggestion of helping her with her aerobics also fails.

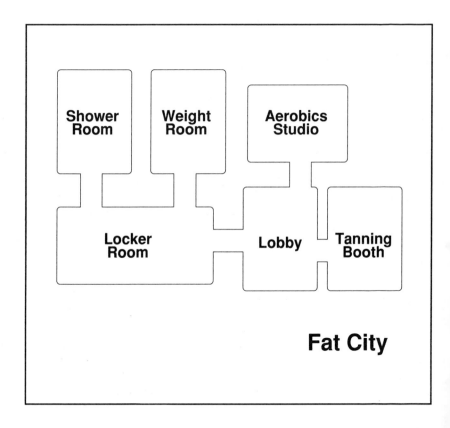

Fat City

Score: 1000 of 4000   Leisure Suit Larry 3

The only reason for this is his physical condition. So he leaves Bambi, all the while telling her how glad he would be to help her - and goes to the locker room. 1000 points

Larry can't believe the size of the locker room. Since he's using Suzi's membership card, he also has to use her locker. But where is it?

Al Lowe, experienced Sierra-Online programmer, built in a little help (suited, of course, to Larry's abilities). Have Larry say "Find the locker." You (and Larry) should interpret the answer like a child's game: "You burn your fingers at the goal."

Larry has to open the locker when he finds it. You must use a combination instead of a key to unlock it. Three numbers will do the trick. However Suzi didn't give Larry the combination. Obviously he'll have to figure out the combination himself, but how? "Wait a minute, maybe she wrote it down...," thinks Larry. Sure enough: the combination is written on one of the items he picked up in his inventory.

The only problem is that it's written in a code as if it was kept in a Swiss bank account. The solution is really simple: have Larry look in "Nontoonyt Tonite". The numbers are listed next to the page numbers in the table of contents. 1068 points

The Larry Story

What man of Larry's caliber hasn't dreamed of exploring the secrets in a woman's purse? Looking through the locker of a young lady lawyer is just as good, isn't it? Larry sees an idol whom he tries to emulate, deodorant and a woman's sweatsuit. "If you want to do anything here, you'll have to put it on," thinks Larry.
1172 points

Larry enters the weight room which is dominated by a giant weight lifting machine. That will cost you a lot of sweat, Larry. He stays by the side of the machine facing the door. There's a machine for doing leg curls. Instruct Larry to use the machine. As he obediently obeys, you're challenged to do the same (maybe to keep you from nodding off?).

You don't need to do this more than 14 times because you may get strained ligaments.

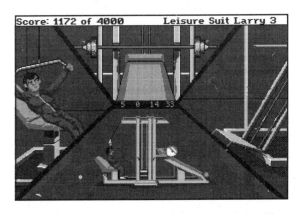

The next exercise is the bench press. Once again you are challenged to do the exercises along with Larry. ("Exercise-Along-With Larry.")

The next exercise uses a rope. Larry has to pull a heavy weight. Once again, you are asked to ....

Fortunately the last exercise on the front of the machine is an easy one. Lift your body off the ground and slowly let it down again. 14 repetitions of this exercise are child's play.

There's still hope for tonight, Larry. After the exercises are finished, you'll witness the spectacle of the famous, well-known Pulsating Pectorals. At the

end of the exercises, Larry has lost all of the weight he gained and has even added a few muscles to his frame. He now looks acceptable for his age.
1272 points

He returns to the locker room, opens his locker and takes off Suzi's sweatsuit. Now Larry is naked. You did remember to bring Larry's souvenir from his encounter with Tawnie, didn't you? Use WEAR to have Larry pull it up around his hips. Larry closes the locker before going in the showers.

In the shower you'll notice something unusual. This will help you to control Larry from above. First Larry has to turn on the water and then get under it. If you remembered your provisions, Larry will be able to wash up and get clean. Then Larry turns off the water and leaves the shower.
1332 points

Back in the locker room, he uses the same combination to open up the locker and dry off. Then he tries Suzi's deodorant. He wonders if it will fail like that cheap stuff he bought at the convenience store in Lost Wages. Now he is finished with the exercises and the shower. He puts on his leisure suit and closes the locker.
1381 points

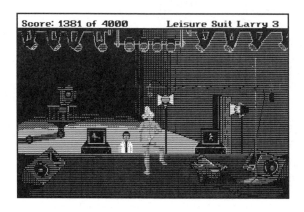

Hungry for action, Larry returns to the Aerobic Studio, where Bambi is still working on herself. Larry has changed so much that she doesn't recognize him. The entire time Larry wants to ask her "Say, how come there's so much video equipment in an Aerobic Studio?"

Bambi tells him about her idea of making a video available worldwide.
She also tells Larry of her troubles. How is her video going to succeed on the
market, what makes her product any different from all of the other aerobic
videotapes? Larry has the answer of course. He was, after all, at one time the
marketing director for Natives Inc. and has proved that he knows what millions
of idiots are capable of buying. Bambi appreciates this and expresses her
gratitude. Larry swallows and does his share.
1439 points

This corresponds exactly to all of the fantasies he had while watching stolen
porno videos. We'll leave him to this pleasure.
1483 points

Hot on Patti's trail

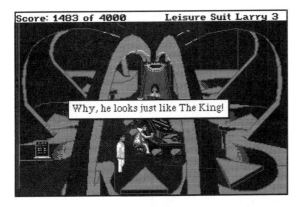

The exercise on
(under) the bench is
barely finished when
Larry remembers
"his" Patti. So off he
goes, to show the
pianist his body of
steel and ask her for a
date. Patti is sitting in
the Casino Lounge
playing the piano.
Maybe you'll see the
King with her...a

subtle hint that Patti is a dream girl. Since neither the King nor Larry want to
talk to each other, Larry sits down next to Patti.

Another conversation starts between Larry and Patti, culminating in Larry's
asking her for a date. What does Patti say? "Yes but a real gentleman," says
Patti, "should always bring a present on the first date." Larry, unfortunately,
doesn't have one. Then he remembers seeing some flowers in a cave. They

would be worthy of a girl like Patti. So he says goodbye once again and sets off to find the flowers.

While looking for the orchids, Larry doesn't even look at the nightclub door, which was closed until now. A lot of orchids are still growing in the cave. He picks as many as he needs. Now he has a typical bride's gift (real orchids!), which not many women receive these days. He races back to Patti.

Just before he enters the Casino Lounge, he remembers another native tradition. He converts them into a South Sea dream. Now he has to hurry and give them to Patti before they wilt. The game of question and answer starts all over again. As he hands her the flowers, Larry thinks to himself that nothing more can go wrong.
1580 points

When she asks him what he wants, he gives her a clear but diplomatic answer. Larry is happy because she has already told him and showed him what is waiting for him in her room. But she wants something else now. Is Larry depressed because he doesn't know where it is or is this a parallel to his experiences in Lost Wages? Regardless, he gets up and starts looking.
1783 points

He doesn't find a mood-inducing drink on the beach. But he spreads out his (oops, Tawnie's) beach towel to get a good suntan. Careful Larry, there's a hole in the ozone!
1813 points

Larry suddenly remembers, wasn't a drink included in the admission to that boring show? Did he drink the bottle of wine? Or was it still there? It can't hurt to look, he thinks. Sure enough, the bottle is exactly where he left it. Now he can take it back to Patti's room.
1828 points

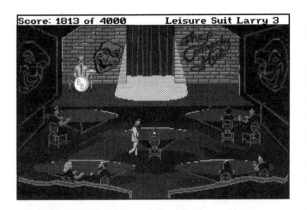

Score: 1813 of 4000   Leisure Suit Larry 3

He rushes into the hotel lobby and presses the up button on the elevator. Larry discovers that there are lots of floors (what a surprise!). As far as he knows, Patti lives in the penthouse on the top floor. The elevator starts moving as soon as he pushes the button. Finally he reaches the top. Patti stretches out on the bed and they talk a little. He places the bottle of wine on the tray next to the glasses.
1870 points

Now begins the tender story of Patti and Larry. They look into each other's eyes and make love to the music of Ravel's Bolero (what else would a pianist listen to?). The following scenes are automatic, so that nobody pushes the wrong button in the heat of...

Larry's dreams of love, happiness and partnership are destroyed by one word from Patti. "Arnold", she whispers, as they fall asleep after passionate lovemaking. Larry is deeply wounded,"If she's thinking of someone else while we're making love, then I'm not going to stick around. That's it with women. I'm going where there aren't any women, where there can't be any more disappointments like this." He leaves the suite. Patti stretches out to hold Larry's arm. But he's gone. Patti, not knowing what she said, doesn't know what happened. When she looks, from her balcony, for him she sees him walking through the impenetrable bamboo jungle.

Now, it's your turn. Patti, as we know, is a modern girl - she starts looking for Larry. Your responsibility is to help her find him.
2332 points

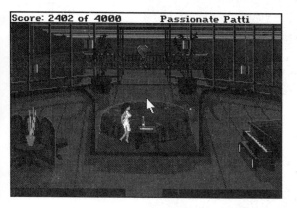

Patti has to change clothes before she starts looking. It's very unwise to go into any jungle in a negligee. You have to describe what Patti puts on. If you take a look around at what is lying there you may have an easier time. While she is getting dressed, take another look to see if anything was hidden. Remember all the things a man needs to remove from a woman when he is undressing her. And remember to have Patti put back on all of those things.
2402 points

Take a final look around before Patti leaves. Maybe there's something she can take with her on her long, exhausting search. As soon as Patti has everything she needs, she goes to the elevator and rides to the ground floor.
2427 points

Patti has an idea of how difficult it will be to find Larry. To equip herself for the search, she picks up different things on the way.

These things are related to her work. She finds a little magic lantern and takes it with her.

Since her search for Larry takes her into the jungle, she brings items necessary for survival in the jungle. Looking in the "Nontoonyt Tonite" helps her decide what she needs.
2539 points

In her search for Larry, Patti comes to places that have been closed until now. It's obvious that the entertainment in these places is great. As usual there is a maitre'd at the door who wants to put in his two cents.
2582 points

Although Patti is very impressed with Dale's show, as soon as she gets the chance, she wants to ask him about her Larry and how to get through the impenetrable bamboo jungle. Dale means well, but it's hard to understand his clue. Again, you have to study "Nontoonyt Tonite". The solution is in the song (singing it won't help). The only signs in the jungle are East (right), West (left), North (above) and South (below).
2583 points

The jungle

There's not much to say about crossing the bamboo jungle. If Patti didn't have her supplies with her and if she didn't use them, her search would come to a quick end.

2603 points

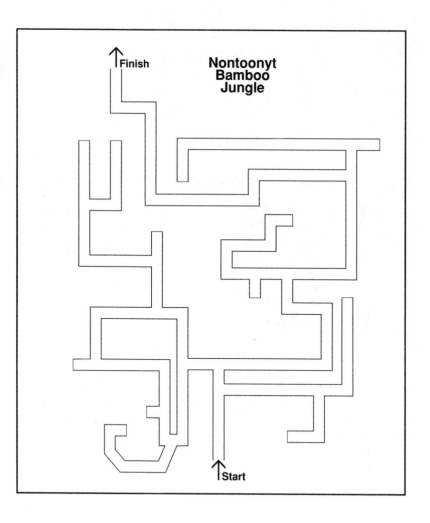

She can avoid getting lost with the song about "Nectarines". The following map will help her get through the jungle even faster.

Getting over the cliff

Patti is hardly out of the bamboo jungle when she comes to the banks of a river. She takes a drink and marches on.

2745 points

Farther along the way she runs into a peculiar rock over the river. The river is flowing so quickly that it's impossible to swim in it. Sure enough, it's a cliff. The river flows over the edge of the cliff. After running around for a while, Patti realizes that the only way to go is down. All of her efforts to find help are doomed to fail. Bushropes grow in the jungle, not on cliffs....

Patti looks down at herself and remembers all of the wonderful things that are promised in commercials. (If you get stuck here, try turning on the afternoon commercials and study the commercials that are aimed at women.) After a few contortions - after all, there are a lot of people watching - Patti is holding the necessary item in her hands.

2760 points

Now she begins to carefully descend the cliff. After swinging back and forth for a while, it turns out that manufacturers don't always tell the truth about their products in commercials. It's a long way down....

The bridge over the canyon

Patti struggles to her feet. Dazed by her fall, she looks around and sees the wild remains of Dr. Nonookee's private garden. The strange weeds remind her of forbidden things that "nice" girls are supposed to avoid. Well, it won't ruin her reputation if she picks some of them. Patti remembers the sailboats of the natives; they use this weed for fastening things all the time. That's how she'll cross the canyon! It doesn't take her long (directions in "Nontoonyt Tonite") to make it.

2910 points

Score: 2935 of 4000   Passionate ▓▓tti

She looks around before crossing the canyon. While looking, she picks some more fruit. What do these two hairy round things remind her of? Then she makes like a cowboy with a lasso. After finally landing it, she can start climbing. But first she must secure the other end. Some of her clothing is giving her trouble. There's only one thing to do: tear off what you don't need and away we go...

3025 points

Exploring unknown paths

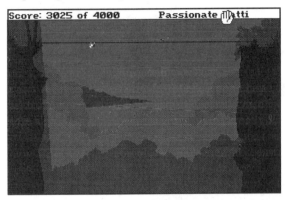

After crossing the canyon, Patti has to go through dangerous, unknown territory. (Even players with fast reflexes should save as often as possible!) The first creature Patti meets is a ferocious wild boar. Patti has to resort to more cowboy tactics, similar to what cowboys use to stop bulls, to keep the animal at arm's length. She can only make the weapon she needs with another piece of clothing, which has room for the two missiles that she picked up. When the boar attacks, she throws her bola around the boars legs. He falls into the river, never to be seen again.
3175 points

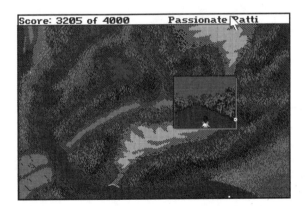

The path to the river is now free. Since there is no other path, Patti must go through or in the water. Look carefully and you will find the equipment she needs. Patti must push it into the middle of the river before climbing on top of it.
3205 points

The stream carries Patti into an adventure. She rides the waves as if she were on a motorcycle. You can see Patti's position on a map. Again, save as often as possible. And don't get discouraged, you CAN do it. Take a look at the map. It's not very creative (about high school level).

The reunion
Before Patti finds a good place to go ashore she is taken captive by cannibalistic Amazons. Once in the cage, she senses the presence of another human being. Did they really find each other? Yes, but the fire is already burning under the cauldron. The only thing that will help here is magic. Full of confidence, Patti tries all of her magic and creates a magical door.
3855 points

They escape to a studio where there are a few (pleasant) surprises waiting for them. Patti needs to take action one more time after a machine throws them up in the air. She manages to zap the machine off. Then they meet Roberta Williams.
3895 points

This takes care of their future life. It ends with the beginning, as Larry asks "his" Patti "Give me the name of a bar". "Lefty's". "I have to go see if my hero can get in there." You'll be laughing when you read this on the screen and will be looking forward to the adventure Larry has in Lefty's Bar. Or you'll be wondering which part of the never ending story you still remember.

5.   Complete Solutions to all of the Programs

Note: In this chapter you'll find the complete solutions to all three Leisure Suit Larry games.

How to use the solutions
Don't expect these solutions to be as detailed as the explanations found in software manuals. This isn't the purpose of this book or the Leisure Suit Larry games. The attraction of the Leisure Suit Larry games is discovering for yourself what you can do and which move to make next.

So, read this chapter only after you've exhausted all the possibilities you can think of and you (as Larry) aren't making progress. The solution will be listed in three columns, the first is the location, the second is the action to be taken and the third is the total number of points earned.

Leisure Suit Larry 1:
In the Land of the Lounge Lizards

We need to tell you one time saving trick before Leisure Suit Larry 1 begins. Since it can become tedious answering the five questions that verify your age each time you load Leisure Suit Larry, Al Lowe designed a trick to skip this procedure. When the first question appears, simultaneously press <Alt><X> to abort the procedure and jump right into the program. Also, as you may have discovered, don't enter an age under 18 years.

Objects in Larry's Inventory

1. Wallet
Any man about town carries this standard equipment. If Larry loses it or gives it away, he'll end up in all types of trouble.

2. Breath Spray
Standard equipment, Larry just can't live without his breath spray. He needs to use his breath spray often. Without it, Larry has little chance with his dream ladies.

3. Pocket Lint
Standard equipment. According to conservative estimates, this can be found in every pants pocket in the Western world. Lint, as you know, is pretty useless.

4. Wrist Watch
Standard equipment. Normally the right brand of wrist watch is easily converted into quick cash anywhere in the world. However, this doesn't apply to Larry's wristwatch since it came from a box of Cracker Jacks®. In Lost Wages, the only thing it will do for Larry is tell time.

5. Apple
Classic tool of seduction (providing a snake isn't present). It's an old tradition in Lost Wages to give an apple to anyone who has lost his shirt. Then that person is supposed to sell the apple. Be friendly if a poor unfortunate soul, who is trying to sell an apple, approaches you outside the casino.

6. Diamond Ring
There are two types of women (aside from all the other types). The first are women who lose expensive diamond rings in men's room sinks in shady bars. The second are the type who want to get married immediately after a man gives them a diamond ring.

7. Glass of Whiskey
Available all over the world for a small price. It's very masculine to carry an open shot glass of whiskey as you walk around. The glass of whiskey will help you make friends with old drunks.

8. Remote Control
Perfect for switching between sports shows without getting up from the sofa. This is the best way to operate a television set that has a broken on/off knob (pliers also work but Larry doesn't have a pair of pliers). Sometimes a grateful drunk will help you find a remote control.

9. Rose
A rose is a rose is a rose is a rose....even if you find one in a dimly lit hallway of a shady bar. You can use it in the disco to put a girl in a friendly mood.

10. Prophylactic
Required for protection from AIDS. Popularly referred to as "lubbers" by sales clerks who are not experts in this area. Prophylactics are available in various styles, sizes and colors at convenience stores in Lost Wages.

11. Used Prophylactic
Never use one a second time. It'll get Larry in plenty of trouble if he doesn't get rid of it when he's finished.

12. Box of Candy
Along with roses and diamond rings, a box of candy will warm a lady's heart. With some ladies, though, you have to get out the heavy artillery and place a rose and a diamond ring on top of the box of candy. Unfortunately, candy isn't for sale in Lost Wages. You have to steal it. Where? Sometimes you'll find a box on a table in certain ladies' bedrooms.

13. Inflatable Doll
These are found in the funniest places (for example, in closets). If you find one of these, blow it up and try it out, even if you have second thoughts. After all, you should try everything once.

14. Disco Pass
Guaranteed way to get into a disco. Because not everyone wants to watch bears fight, some people throw their passes away in the strangest places, for example, in the casino where other people throw something else away.

15. Pocket Knife
All real men use pocket knives. Sometimes, if you make friends with him first, an old drunk will give you one.

16. Bottle of Wine
Almost as good as whiskey but one rule concerning wine that Larry should know: Never take a bottle of wine into a taxi. It's a deadly decision. However, there is no better way to make friends with an old drunk. You can count on receiving something in return. Available in any good convenience store.

17. "Jugs" Magazine

The issue this month features not only a nice centerfold but informative articles, such as how professional window washers secure themselves to buildings. Available at any good convenience store.

18. Hammer

Can be found in the most unusual places, for example in trash bins. Building contractors and police agree that a hammer is a useful tool for breaking glass.

19. Bottle of Pills

Be careful with a bottle of pills if you're uncertain what the pills will do. The same pill may make one person very excited but have no effect on another. The most interesting pill bottles are always just out of reach. You need to read articles in magazines in order to discover ways to reach the pill bottles.

20. Rope

Used in all adventure movies (and adventure games). Used in Lost Wages, too. It's the only way to properly tie yourself up. Try your best to take the rope whenever you see it.

The Sierra Adventure Game Interpreter

Complex adventure games that include animated graphics are at times frustrating. If you've become so frustrated that you want to throw the program disk (no matter how frustrated you are, NEVER throw your computer!) at the wall, you should know of one trick we found in Leisure Suit Larry 1. You wouldn't even have an opportunity to do use this trick if Sierra-Online (or Al Lowe, the programmer) hadn't made one small (but beneficial) mistake.

This mistake allows you to call the Adventure Game Interpreter at anytime. This interpreter is similar to an editor and allows you to move through the program just like a programmer.

You can also call certain options, from the Adventure Game Interpreter, that don't appear in the normal menus. The following list of commands and results are, to the best of our knowledge, complete. (We didn't ask Al Lowe, though.)

Solutions

Since we tested the Adventure Game Interpreter on a current version, we can't guarantee that Sierra won't release future versions without this option. We weren't able to discover a way of calling the Adventure Game Interpreter on either Leisure Suit Larry 2 or Leisure Suit Larry 3 so we assume they do not contain this option.

Press <Alt><D> simultaneously and then <Enter> or <Return> twice to activate the Adventure Game Interpreter. After you've finished using the Interpreter, press <Alt><D> to switch it off.

The following is a list of commands you can enter with the Adventure Game Interpreter:

Keyboard Commands	
<Alt><X>	Cancel startup questions
<Alt><D>	Activate Game editor
<Alt><V>	
<Alt><P>	Shows where Larry can walk
<Alt><E>	Display coordinates of Larry
<Alt><I>	Information about objects
<Alt><Z>	Abort game
<Alt><M>	Heapsize
<Scroll Lock>	Shows program lines

Text commands for input line (while in editor)	
object number	Lists object number and object
room number	Shows x/y coordinates and room number of Larry as he moves on the screen.
get all	You can add to Larry's inventory with this command. To use the correct object number, first use the OBJECT NUMBER command to see the object and its corresponding number.
object room	Use to determine location of an object. For example, enter 1 (wallet). The location is 255 (Larry).

We hope that this list will provide new ways for you to enjoy playing Leisure Suit Larry 1.

The Solution

In front of the Bar	open door	
In the Bar	sit down	
	order whiskey	1
	get up	
Bathroom hallway	talk to man	
	give whiskey	3
	take rose	4
	open door	
Toilet	sit	5
	get up	
	read wall (4 times)	7
	look at sink	
	take ring	10
In front of the Bar	call cab	
	enter	
In Taxi	store	
	pay	
	get out	11
Liquor Store	take magazine	12
	take wine	13
	buy prophylactic	
In front of the store	give wine	22
	look at phone	23
	use phone	25
	call cab	
In Taxi	bar	
In the Bar	knock on door	
	Ken sent me	
Behind the door	turn TV on with remote control	28
	switch channel (6 times)	36
Room above the Bar	undress	
	use lubber	46
	get in bed	57
	remove lubber	58
	take candy	60
	open window	
	climb through window	

Solutions

Trash bin	take hammer	63
	climb out	
Taxi	Casino	
Casino	use slot machine	
	or play blackjack	
Lobby	look in ashtray	
	take card	64
Taxi	disco	
At the Disco	show pass	69
In the Disco	sit down	70
	look at girl	
	talk to girl	71
	ask her to dance	76
	sit down	
	talk to girl	
	give her candy	81
	give her rose	86
	give her ring	91
	give her money	98
Taxi	chapel	
Chapel	marry girl	110
In front of the Casino	buy apple	113
Casino	(replace money)	
Elevator	four	
4th Floor	knock door	
Room	turn radio on	114
	talk to girl	
Taxi	Shop	
In front of the Store	answer phone	119
	use phone	
	order wine	124
Room	lie down on bed	
	cut rope with knife	134
	take rope	137
Casino	Replace money	
Taxi	bar	
Room above the Bar	climb out of window	
Balcony	tie rope round waist	
	fasten rope to railing	
	climb over railing	

	smash window with hammer	
	take pills	145
	climb back	
	untie rope	
Taxi	casino	
Casino, 8th Floor	look at girl	
	talk to girl (repeatedly)	
	give her pills	150
	look at desk	
	push button	
	(get in elevator)	155
Penthouse Closet	take doll	160
	blow up doll	165
	use doll (2*)	
	>>>Animated sequence<<<	173
Penthouse Balcony	jump into tub	
	look at girl	
	talk to girl	
	look at girl	
	give her apple	188
	>>>Animated sequence<<<	21

Leisure Suit Larry 2:
Looking for Love (In Several Wrong Places)

Objects in Larry's Inventory

Dollar Bill

If you're thrown out of the house and you don't have a dollar bill in your pocket, you should try very hard to find one. Usually the dollar will be in the pocket of a pair of pants that you are not wearing. Of course, the pants aren't where they're supposed to be either. Maybe they're in the garage.

Lottery Ticket

The dollar bill can quickly become a building block to a new fortune. You have to take a risk and gamble the dollar. On the lottery. One ticket, one dollar. Available in liquor stores.

Cruise Ticket

Essential for taking a cruise. But who wants to do that? Only people who win a cruise on a television game show should do it. Why try to win a cruise? For Larry, the reason is obvious: Girls, Girls, Girls (and we don't mean the movie starring Elvis Presley).

Million Dollar Bill

Has both advantages and disadvantages. The advantage: It saves a lot of counting when you want to pay the winner his one million dollar prize. Disadvantage: It's incredibly difficult to get change for one of these. In contrast to the one million pound note (Mark Twain), it's not very useful for establishing credit. In Los Angeles, there is no credit. It's easier to spend a million lira bill.

Swimsuit

Necessary on a cruise. Italian swimsuits are popular and attract a lot of attention. The best Italian swimsuits can be purchased only at an original Italian shop. They seem to have converted the price directly from lira into dollars.

The Larry Story

Wad O'Dough
You can always use one of these. Especially if it's a big wad of hundred dollar bills. This is what you get in change if you pay with a million dollar bill.

Passport
You can't leave the country without one of these. It's bad luck to be thrown out of the house without it. There you are without your passport and to make things worse, it gets thrown in the garbage.

Grotesque Gulp
Specialty found in liquor stores in Los Angeles. About the size of a garbage can. Can be transported when it's full. Has saved a lot of castaways from dying of thirst.

Sunscreen
Despite using a protection factor of 2000 against ultraviolet light, Larry just won't tan. Although the sunscreen does prevent sunburn it is not water resistant. After a dip, put some more on. Can be purchased in any drugstore.

Onklunk
Extremely rare. Onklunks are extremely sensitive to changes in temperature and humidity. It's best to store an onklunk, immediately after it's been finished and polished, in an air conditioned safety deposit box in Mexico. This prevents this expensive musical instrument from getting out of tune. Then throw away the key. Be cautious if someone offers you an onklunk. It's usually related to forgery and dark deeds.

Fruit
Great to have around when you're hungry. Passengers on cruise ships usually find a bowl of fruit in their cabin. Most guests take the fruit with them as a souvenir.

Sewing Kit
What would a mother-in-law (or potential mother-in-law) do without a sewing kit? You could either sew some buttons with it or improvise a fishing pole.

Spinach Dip
Spinach makes sailors strong. But spinach dip makes landlubbers sick. Quick, throw it away before it's too late!

Wig
Protects your bald head from sunstroke when your sombrero is missing. Available at the barbershop.

Bikini
Although a beautiful South Sea coral island, it was once an atomic bomb testing site. You can't take it off or take it with you. In fact, it's not seen anywhere simply because bikini doesn't appear in the game.

Bikini Top
Big advantage: Has a habit of getting lost in swimming pools. Big disadvantage: It's not adequate for a disguise.

Bikini Bottom
Strange, this doesn't get lost as much as bikini tops. If you really need one to disguise yourself, you have to search thoroughly. On FKK beach, for example.

Knife
All real men use knives. Larry does too. A knife is an incredibly versatile tool. You can cut all kinds of things with one.

Soap
Usually found lying on the sinks in hotels. Probably because the hotel management values guests who appear to be well-groomed. Most guests take soap with them as a souvenir. Soap is made of the alkali salts of higher fatty acids and has many different uses. You can wash with it and stick several small pieces together and stuff it into all kinds of things to make them curve.

The Larry Story

Matches
Even though the hotel management doesn't value guests who set their rooms on fire, matches are usually found lying on nightstands in hotels. Most guests take matches with them as a souvenir. You can use matches to set fire to lots of things besides hotel rooms. Molotov Cocktails, for example.

Flower
Grows in the jungle. Popular greeting of flower children. Noted for its long lasting, soothing effect on unpleasant companions.

Hair Rejuvenator
Sold at many barbershops. As explosive as a Molotov Cocktail. Do not drink. Doesn't do much for your hair, either.

Suitcase
You can put all kinds of things in one of these: Underwear, shirts, bombs. Nothing against bombs. Have you ever been at the end of a long line and wished that you had one?

Airline Ticket
Available at all airports. You can't get on a plane without one of these. Didn't you know that?

Parachute
Forget those machines selling flight insurance. The best kind of traveller's insurance is a parachute, especially when you're a passenger on a small airline.

Bobby Pin
A traumatic experience for Larry: His mother always scattered bobby pins in the food. Since that time, Larry has had an aversion to eating. You'll recall that he doesn't eat in any of his adventures. He does, however, like to search his food for bobby pins. He saves them. After all, bobby pins are very handy: You can open any lock with one of them.

Solutions

Pamphlet
Sometimes you find these in airports. Although reading them can bore you to death, for some strange reason boring people get extremely excited reading them.

Airsick Bag
Almost every plane has these. The way their pilots fly could make their passengers sick. You'll find an airsick bag in the little pockets on the back of airline seats. There are also people who take these innocent bags with them and use them for something else. Therefore, many airlines issue notices waiving any responsibility for airsick bags that are used to light Molotov Cocktails.

Stout Stick
Nature lovers always carry a stout stick when they travel into unexplored wilderness. You can use a stout stick to defend yourself from giant snakes. Otherwise, these snakes might keep you from getting back home in time for coffee.

Vine
Tropical climbing plant that grows in the jungle. Some reports (and several movies) claim that the Eighteenth Earl of Greystoke enjoyed swinging on them and occasionally used them to make lassos.

Ashes
Inorganic remains of burned animal or plant substances. Many people are fond of putting them in a sackcloth that they wear. You can also spread them on the ground. That's how they make sports stadiums. Don't use it at the skating rink because it dulls the ice surface.

The Solution

Garage	take dollar	3
Space Quest Park	look	
	look girl	4
Yard	look bin	
	look hole	5
Liquor Store	buy ticket	8
Outer Office	show ticket	18
Green Room	sit	19
	get up	
	>>>Animated sequence<<<	45
	sit	
	get up	
	>>>Animated sequence<<<	64
Molto Lira	take swimsuit	69
	pay	72
House	look through trash (2 times)	
	take passport	77
Drug Store	take sunscreen	
	pay for sunscreen	86
Liquor Store	take soda	91
	pay for soda	94
Barber Shop	sit down	
	>>>Animated sequence<<<	97
Music Store	talk to clerk	
	>>>Animated sequence<<<	104
Purser	show ticket	113
Cabin	take fruit	116
	open door	
	(Quickly leave for next cabin)	
	wear swimsuit	
Neighbor's cabin	open nightstand	
	take sewing kit	122
Swimming pool	use sunscreen	125
	sit	128
	(Girl waiting)	
	get up	

	swim	
	take breath	
	dive	
	take top	135
	get out	
	use sunscreen	138
Cabin	wear suit	
Barber Shop	sit down	
	>>>Animated sequence<<<	141
Bar	take spinach dip	143
Command bridge	switch lifeboat timer	149
Upper deck	enter lifeboat	153
	>>>Animated sequence<<<	158
Lifeboat	wear wig	163
	throw away dip	165
	>>>Animated sequence<<<	190
Jungle	pick flowers	193
	>>>Animated sequence<<<	
Restaurant	talk to maitre'd	
	sit down	194
	>>>Animated sequence<<<	195
	take knife	198
Jungle		
Hotel	take matches	200
	take soap	202
Jungle		
Barber Shop	sit down	
	>>>Animated sequence<<<	205
Jungle		
FKK beach	take bikini	209
Jungle		
Restaurant		
Jungle		
Hotel	wear bikini	214
Jungle		
Barber Shop	sit down	
	>>>Animated sequence<<<	217

The Larry Story

Jungle		
Beach		
Jungle		
Restaurant		
Jungle		
Hotel	put soap into bikini top	229
Jungle		
Barber Shop		
Beach		241
Cliff	change clothes	247
In front of Airport	give flowers	254
Barber Shop	look girl	257
	sit down	
	>>>Animated sequence<<<	260
Customs	show passport	265
Baggage pickup	take suitcase	
	>>>Arcade<<<	270
	>>>Animated sequence<<<	285
Ticket lobby	buy ticket	290
Departures	buy insurance	293
	buy food	
	take pin out	300
Gate 1	take pamphlet	311
	show ticket	314
Airplane	give pamphlet to man	324
	take airsick bag	327
	get up	
Airplane tail	wear parachute	331
	open padlock with pin	336
	turn handle	
	open door	342
In the air	use parachute	
Tree	cut harness	350
Jungle	take stick	354
	crawl under bush	360
Jungle 2	use stick	370
Quick sand	>>>Animated sequence<<<	375
Piranha stream	jump (3 times)	
	>>>Animated sequence<<<	381
	take vine	385

Leisure Suit Larry 3:
Passionate Patti in Pursuit of the Pulsating Pectorals

Objects in Larry's Inventory

Credit card
Americans have discovered that nothing can be done these days without one. They arrive in the mail months after you've ordered them.

Sharp knife
Every adventurer uses one of these (Indiana Jones did). Larry also uses one. But how do you get one. It's very easy: You take a dull knife, for example a Ginsu® knife that you can buy anywhere as a souvenir, and sharpen it. Use a wide, flat stone for the best results.

Erotic Sculpture
Specialty of the natives of Nontoonyt. Typically carved out of Granadilla wood. You need a sharp knife, some imagination, but not much talent.

Grass Skirt
Traditional clothing of souvenir vendors on Nontoonyt. As indicated by the name, grass skirts are made out of grass. This grass is difficult to cut, which resulted in the original natives' splitting into two hostile groups: One group tried to sell souvenirs in the nude. The other group developed the art of forging to make sharp knives, so that they could cut the grass, so that they could make grass skirts out of the grass, so that they could wear the grass skirts when they sold souvenirs. The first group became so impoverished they became extinct.

Soap-On-A-Rope
It's very useful when you want to take a shower after working out and don't know where to put the soap. The disadvantage: Hardly anyone appreciates this practical item. Either you get them as Christmas presents where you work or you find them in inconspicuous places such as in dressing room sinks.

500 Dollar Bills

A lot of small change. What you need to guarantee that you will get legal assistance. To get such a pile of small change, it's worth your while to investigate such occupations as singing in bars and public sidewalks or dancing in front of large crowds: The money is waiting.

Land Deed

A deed is needed if you want to give away your land because it's difficult for landowners to carry their land in a briefcase. A great present is a deed to worthless swamp land.

Beach towel

Usually found on hotel beaches. Generally picked up after the hotel guests have left the beach. This rarely happens before the owner has purchased his or her last souvenir. Beach towels are perfect for drying off after working out. (Shame on you if you didn't know that.)

Spa Keycard

Keycards are both membership cards and keys for people who are members of health spas. The key enables members to use the spa whenever they choose, and at the same time keeps non-members out - unless they manage to get hold of the keycard through some stupid coincidence.

Divorce Decree

Can only be obtained with the help of a lawyer. Women, who hold the institution of marriage sacred, love these.

Some Orchids

Although grown wild in tropical regions, orchids made into wreaths are still a popular form of greeting. The natives call them "Leis". Unfortunately, orchids quickly wilt. You can always make a new lei since orchids grow like weeds.

Penthouse Key

You need one to take the elevator to a penthouse. They're hard to get because the owners of these keys carefully guard them and share them with a select few.

Bottle of Wine
They're a very useful tool (when full, of course) for stimulating brand new relationships (see Leisure Suit Larry 1). When empty, they're useful for transporting liquids. Wine is served in all establishments but some places don't serve it until the entertainer finishes his number.

Panties
Not very useful, at least in this game, but they look good and don't hurt anyone.

Pantyhose
You should always carry some with you. There are situations, though not so often anymore, in which it is the only form of acceptable currency. Women use them for protection against the wind and cold. If they're found anywhere that's not windy and cold, for example, on a tropical island, a women can still use them to lower herself down a cliff.

Bra
Binds two round or curved objects together. Usually found in women's hotel rooms and bedrooms. Worn on the body.

Dress
Great for covering up things. In the past, charitable women would tear up their dresses to make bandages for wounded soldiers. Also used in our adventures for the same purpose. Typical of adventure films and games, the women lose more and more of their dresses as the plot unfolds.

Magic Marker
In a tropical paradise, a magic marker could come from a witch doctor. If you're looking for a magic marker, search near charts that contain writing from a magic marker.

Coconuts
Round, brown and hairy. No one knows what the hair is used for. Nor does anyone know much about the nuts. They're to big to fit in a nutcracker. The meat isn't very juicy (but it doesn't have any pits.) One single coconut is too small to scare away wild animals. It would be quite a different story if you bound two of them together and threw them.

Marijuana
Tobacco-like mixture of leaves and blossoms of the female hemp plant of India. If you smoke it, you get a funny, light-headed feeling. If you don't smoke it, you can use it for other things - for example, you could make a rope out of it.

The Larry Story

The Solution

Vantage point	use binoculars	2
	read plaque	4
House	>>>Animated sequence<<<	
Jungle 2	>>>Animated sequence<<<	
Firm	>>>Animated sequence<<<	
Jungle 1	Take wood	6
House	open mailbox	
	look into mailbox	
	take envelope	26
Beach	look at girl	
	talk to girl (3 times)	
	give her credit card	48
	>>Animated sequence<<	116
TV room	turn on TV	
	sit on bench	
	take paper	
	read paper	
	stand up	
Fountain	look at stairs	
	sharpen knife on stairs	166
	carve wood	216
In front of Chip'n'Dales	cut grass with knife	236
	make skirt	266
Dressing Room	wear skirt	276
Beach	>>>Animated sequence<<<	311
Show Lobby	show ticket	
	give 20 Dollars	
	>>>Animated sequence<<<	361
Foyer	(wait, until Cherry appears)	
	look at girl	
	talk to girl	366
	offer land	391
	stop looking	
Office	ask for deed	401
Office	sit down	
	ask for deed	431
	Leave lawyers office	

Comedy hut	sit down	
	>>>Animated sequence<<<	
	get up	531
Office	ask for deed	551
Foyer	knock on door	576
	>>>Animated sequence<<<	576
	dance	619
On the way	look mirror	621
Office	talk to Roger	
	Answer yes to the question	
	by giving him $500	631
	>>>Animated sequence<<	731
	talk Roger	
Showroom Stage	wear suit	756
Casino Lounge	sit	
	look Patti	
	talk Patti	761
	make a date	
	leave Patti	
Office	ask for divorce decree	781
	look at decree	881
	show keycard to Roger	
Casino Lounge	sit	
	look Patti	
	talk Patti	
	make a date	
	show decree	981
	make date	
	leave Patti	
Cabana	turn water on	983
	take soap	995
Beach	take towel	997
Fat City,		
Aerobic Studio	open door with keycard	1000
	look girl	
	talk girl	
	leave girl	
Lobby	open door	1003

Locker Room	find locker	
	turn keycard	1068
	open door	1168
	wear sweats	1172
	close locker	
Weight Room	use leg curl	
	get up	
	use bench press	
	get up	
	use pullup	
	get up	
	use bar pull	
	get up	
	>>>Animated sequence<<<	1172
Locker Room	open locker	
	wear towel	
	close locker	
Shower	turn water on	
	use soap	1332
	turn water off	
Locker Room	open locker	
	use towel	1354
	Use deodorant	1381
	wear suit	
	close locker	
	look girl	
	talk girl	
	talk girl	
	talk girl	
	help girl with video	1439
	>>>Animated sequence<<<	1483
Piano Bar	sit	
	look at girl	
	talk girl	
	make date	
	stop looking	
Cave	pick orchids	1508
Hotel Floor	make lei	1558

Solutions

Piano Bar	sit down	
	look at girl	
	give her lei	1580
	make a date	1680
	>>>Animated sequence<<<	
	get up	1783
Beach	spread towel	1813
Chip'n'Dales	take bottle	1828
Hotel Lobby	push button	
Elevator	look button 9	1832
Penthouse	drop wine	1870
	>>>Animated sequence<<<	
	>>>Animated sequence ends<<<	2332
	wear bra	2352
	wear panties	2372
	wear pantyhose	2392
	wear gown	2402
	take bottle	2427
Elevator	press 1	
Piano Bar	take glass	2452
	take marker	2502
Locker Room	fill bottle	2539
	drink water	
In front of Chip'n'Dales	talk to man	
	give tips	2582
Chip'n'Dales	sit down	
	talk to Dale	
	look at Dale	2583
	talk to Dale	
	stop looking	
	get up	
Jungle	drink water	2603
Way:	North, North, East, East,	
	North, West, North, East,	
	North, North, North, West,	
	West, South, West, West,	
	North, North, West, North	2703
River	drink water	2745

Cliff	remove pantyhose	2760
	tie pantyhose to rock	2775
	>>>Animated sequence<<<	2800
Rocky Ledge	take pot	2810
	make rope	2910
	climb palm tree	
	look	
	look up	
	look nuts	
	pick coconuts	2935
	climb down	
	throw rope over canyon	2955
	tie rope to tree	2975
	rip dress	3025
	climb rope	
	>>>Animated sequence<<<	
Jungle	remove bra	3030
	put coconuts into bra	3075
	throw bra at pig	3175
River	move log into water	3185
	sit on log	3205
	>>>Arcade<<<	
	>>>Animated sequence<<<	
Cannibal Cage	use magic marker	3845
	>>>Animated sequence<<<	
Space Quest	Studio unplug wire	3885
	>>>Animated sequence<<<	4000

6. Technical Notes

This section contains answers to many technical questions you might have. There are also some tips on protecting your computer system from computer viruses, playing the game on floppy disks, computer configuration and sound cards.

Using Leisure Suit Larry on your PC or compatible

We're not going to repeat the familiar complaints concerning the PCs lack of music and graphic capabilities. Sierra has managed to "liven up" computer games with its Leisure Suit Larry games.

Virus Alert

Larry uses common sense to protect himself from dangerous and deadly viral infections in his encounters with various people. You should use the same common sense to protect your computer system from computer viruses located on disks you insert into your computer system. If your Leisure Suit Larry is a Sierra factory original and you break the shrinkwrap yourself, you will never have a problem.

Computer viruses are self-replicating programs that can destroy your data and possibly even your hard disk. Virus programs are usually destructive and an infected system can be a nightmare of lost data and disk crashes. Virus programmers like to place their destructive virus programs on "pirated" copies of popular game software. Virus programmers do this so their virus program will get the widest possible distribution in the shortest time.

Therefore we strongly recommend that you never accept copies of the Larry games from anyone. Always use backup copies of the original program disks to start the Larry games! Only use backup copies you have made yourself from the original program disks. This is the only reliable method of protecting your computer system from a virus infestation. Remember that virus programmers like to place their nasty programming creations on popular game disks. Protect your important data, know where your disks have been! The best way to protect yourself against a computer virus is to use the original program disks.

Altering files

Be very careful if you're planning to make changes, such as deleting or changing files, to your version of the Leisure Suit Larry games. For example, in an attempt to delete the music beginning the PC version of Leisure Suit Larry 3, we replaced the standard sound driver (STD.DRV) in the subdirectory with an empty file. We believed that the music wouldn't play if nothing was available in the driver. However, this turned out to be false. Sierra-Online's games try to get the most out of the sound capabilities of the PC speaker. The games interfered with the system so much that the CMOS-RAM (random access memory) of our PC was deleted. This is where the AT stores all of the system setup information. After this happened our AT didn't recognize drives, graphic cards, or even the hard disk. Everything had to be reconfigured. It's best to make a backup of the data before changing the Sierra data files, especially if you're unfamiliar with your system.

Configuring your system

PCs or compatibles that have one or two disk drives can still load Leisure Suit Larry games. Make backup copies of the original disks as described in your manual. To protect your computer system from computer viruses , never accept copies of the Larry games from anyone!

Configuring Leisure Suit Larry 2

Leisure Suit Larry 2 has been significantly expanded compared to the first version. Not only does Leisure Suit Larry 2 have a higher graphic resolution and support sound but the game files are also much more complex. You'll notice this immediately by the number of disks that are included. However, you must remember a few things.

A number of different files are open during the game. To do this, you must configure your operating system accordingly. Use the CONFIG.SYS file to do this. In order to play Leisure Suit Larry 2 properly, you must either create a CONFIG.SYS file or alter your existing CONFIG.SYS file.

Boot your computer with your system disk and start your computer. Owners of laptop PCs and compatibles must follow the same procedure. The only difference is that the CONFIG.SYS file is usually on a simulated drive in the computer's memory. After starting your laptop computer, try switching to drive C. Otherwise it's the same as operating a desktop PC system.

Enter DIR to see a list of the files. Create a CONFIG.SYS file if you don't see one. Enter the following lines (press <ENTER> or <RETURN> at the end of each line):

```
COPY CON CONFIG.SYS
FILES = 15
<F6>
```

After you press <F6>, the following message will appear:

```
1 File(s) copied
```

Now your system is configured and you must restart your computer with the system disk containing the CONFIG.SYS file.

If your system disk already has a CONFIG.SYS file, you have to check whether the file contains the line:

```
FILES =
```

Use a DOS command to check this. Insert the system disk into the drive and enter:

```
TYPE CONFIG.SYS
```

Press <ENTER> or <RETURN> at the end of the line and the CONFIG.SYS file will display a list on the screen. Check whether there is an entry for FILES. The total has to be 15 or higher.

If there is no entry in FILES or if the entry is smaller than 15, complete the file as follows:

Call the DOS editor with:

EDLIN CONFIG.SYS <ENTER> (<RETURN>)

You can use a different ASCII editor. Usually this is easier than working with EDLIN. If your system cannot find the editor, the following error message will appear:

No command or filename found

In this case you have to use DIR to search your system disk for the EDLIN.EXE file. After you find it, insert the disk in drive A and enter the following command:

EDLIN B:CONFIG.SYS <ENTER> (<RETURN>)

Even if you only have one drive, DOS will automatically switch to it and simulate a B drive. Then you will be prompted to insert a disk for drive B. Insert the system disk containing the CONFIG.SYS file.

After loading the file, EDLIN will respond with an asterisk. Enter the letter "L" to list the contents of the file on the screen. Remember the number that appears next to the FILES entry. Now, if you enter this line, the editor will call it so that you can re-enter it. Then enter:

FILES = 15 <ENTER> (<RETURN>)

If there wasn't an existing FILES entry in the CONFIG.SYS, enter the command:

li

This causes a line to be inserted before the first line. Then enter:

FILES = 15

Then save, with the letter "e", the file you have just finished changing or creating. To continue the installation, first restart your computer with the CONFIG.SYS.

Installing the Larry Games

Starting with Leisure Suit Larry 2, DISK#1 includes INSTALL.EXE, which is the installation program. First make copies of your original disk and use only these copies. Store the originals in a safe place.

Use only copies that you have personally made of the original program disks to protect your computer system from a possible computer virus. Practice Safe Computing just as you would practice Safe Sex. You never know where some disks have been.

Start the installation procedure as outlined in the manual. The Sierra installation programs are very user friendly and make installing the programs a breeze. Follow the instructions displayed on the screen to install the game on your system.

The files of the PC and compatible version

Some of the files included in Leisure Suit Larry games can be deleted if you run out of disk space.

Leisure Suit Larry 1

_INSTALL	BAT	Batch used to install game
LL	COM	Command file for the game
AGI		Program file
AGIDATA	OVL	Program file
CGA_GRAF	OVL	CGA graphic overlay
JR_GRAG	OVL	Graphic overlay for PC Jr.
EGA_GRAF	OVL	EGA and VGA graphic card overlay
HGC_GRAF	OVL	Hercules graphic card overlay
VG_GRAF	OVL	Graphic overlay for PC and compatibles
IBM_OBJS	OVL	Object file for IBM graphic (CGA, EGA, VGA)
HGC_OBJS	OVL	Object file for Hercules graphic card
HGC_FONT		Screen fonts for Hercules graphic card
LOGDIR		Program file
PICDIR		Program file
VIEWDIR		Program file
SNDDIR		Program file
OBJECT		Program file
WORDS	TOK	Program file
VOL	0	Program file
VOL	1	Program file
VOL	2	Program file

First, find out which graphic cards your PC uses. Any graphic drivers in your configuration that you don't need can be deleted from this list.

—————— *Technical* ——————

Leisure Suit Larry 2

There is a big difference between Leisure Suit Larry 1 and the other Leisure
Suit Larry adventures concerning development. When Leisure Suit Larry 1
came out, the first VGA cards in IBM-PS/2 models had just become available.
For this reason, the game was designed for an EGA high resolution graphic
card. In Leisure Suit Larry 2, they changed the game editor so that VGA
graphics could also be supported. In addition, the PC also could support sound
by using special drivers that controlled the most important sound cards. The
structure of the files also changed. You can now change parts of the
installation after Leisure Suit Larry is installed. Also, you can delete the
following files that you no longer nee, from Leisure Suit Larry 2:

Auxiliary programs
INSTALL	EXE	Installation program
__INSTH	BAT	

Graphic drivers
EGA320	DRV	EGA graphic card
MCGA320	DRV	MCGA graphic card (IBM PS/2 30)
TANDY320	DRV	Graphic driver for Tandy computers
PCJR320	DRV	Graphic driver for PC Jr.
CGA320C	DRV	CGA graphics card
CGA320BW	DRV	CGA graphics card, black and white screens
HERCMONO	DRV	Hercules monochrome graphics card

Sound drivers
STD	DRV	Standard PC sound drivers
JR	DRV	Sound driver for PC Jr.
ADL	DRV	Ad-Lib music card
IMF	DRV	IBM PC music feature card
MT32	DRV	Roland MT 32 sound module
CMS	DRV	Additional drivers installed for game blaster card
PATCH	101	

Keyboard drivers

IBMKBD	DRV	For IBM compatible PC
TANDYKBD	DRV	For Tandy PCs
JOYSTICK	DRV	For using a joystick

Program files

EXISTS	COM	Test program
SIERRA	COM	Start game
SCIV	EXE	Game interpreter
RESOURCE	MAP	Program file
RESOURCE	001	Program file
RESOURCE	CFG	Current configuration
RESOURCE	002	Program file
LSL2	QA	Copyright text
RESOURCE	003	Program file
RESOURCE	004	Program file
RESOURCE	005	Program file
RESOURCE	006	Program file

Saved games:

LSL2SG	DIR	Title of files in Leisure Suit Larry
LSL2SG	000	Filename for first saved game
LSL2SG	001	Filename for second saved game
LSL2SG	002	Filename for third saved game
LSL2SG	003	Filename for fourth saved game
		and so on until 10 games are saved in the directory.

The current configuration is saved in the RESOURCE.CFG file. You can use the DOS TYPE command or an editor to view or change this file. It's better to execute any changes in the configuration from the INSTALL.EXE file.

Leisure Suit Larry 3

There aren't any drastic changes in the structure of the files in Leisure Suit Larry 3. This version supports one additional sound card than Leisure Suit Larry 2. Here's a list of the new files:

Sound drivers

CMS	DRV	Creative music system/game blaster
FB01	DRV	Yamaha FB-01 FM sound generator
MT540	DRV	Casiotone MT-540/CT-460
CSM1	DRV	Casio CSM-1 sound module

Auxiliary files

README	COM	Read program
README	TXT	Current instructions

Program files

LARRY3	DRV	Current driver adaptation

Sound with a PC

Isn't it frustrating when you're excited about something new and when you tell your friends about it they already know more about it than you do?

This is what happens to some Leisure Suit Larry players. Just when you're accustomed to playing a game with movable graphics, you discover that it's also possible to play the game with sound. Owners of either an Atari ST or an Amiga won't have any problems adding sound. The ST, capable of producing music, contains a MIDI interface which enables you to hook up a musical device to play the music that accompanies Leisure Suit Larry games. All you need are loudspeakers if you're using an Amiga.

PCs are somewhat different. Sound wasn't even considered for PCs when they were first developed. The only thing that was required was a small loudspeaker for the beeper so that it could indicate errors. The first sound generator programs arrived at about the same time as the PCs.

Then, following the development of expansion slots, IBM developed the IBM sound card. These cards, which were too expensive for the average user, were later followed by the sound cards created by the Roland company.

According to Sierra, the Roland card was developed so that it would be possible to support MIDI interfaces on IBM PCs as well. Bob Siebenberg of the rock group Supertramp composed some of the sound portions for various Sierra games. When the Ad-Lib card came out for a couple of hundred dollars, which was within the normal user's price range, people started to become interested in the capabilities of creating synthesized music. So it isn't surprising that game manufacturers recognized the same opportunities.

Sierra quickly began selling drivers that could also control other sound cards. Leisure Suit Larry 2 and Leisure Suit Larry 3 contain numerous animated sequences. These film sequences, used with a sound card, are similar to the sound and motion of a movie. The newer cards offer the same or similar features at more reasonable prices.

Sound Card Installation

Sierra found a wonderful solution to installing sound for the Leisure Suit Larry 2 and Leisure Suit Larry 3 games. You'll be prompted to select which sound option you want to use as you proceed through the installation procedure.

It's slightly more difficult to install an actual sound card in your computer. IBM PC, AT and compatible computers enable you to stockpile PC capabilities via expansion cards.

Sound cards are a type of expansion card. Before you buy one, you should know as much about your system as possible. Some PC compatibles won't accept any expansion cards so you're forced to use an expansion chassis, which provides slots for expansion cards.

The next problem has to do with the type of slot. As a rule, todays PC and compatible computers have several slots. Several or sometimes all of the slots are reserved: serial ports, parallel ports, graphic adapters, hard disk controllers, RAM expansion, and others.

One important note about sound cards: Carefully read the guarantee or warranty accompanying the card. Some guarantees and warranties are voided if the user installs the card. A dealer may have to install the sound card for you.

We didn't have any problems either adding or operating a sound card. However, be sure you have enough cable and plugs. For example, you'll need a longer cable and special plugs if you want to connect the card to your stereo system.

Characteristics of Sound Cards

You'll find the sound cards supported in Leisure Suit Larry 2 and Leisure Suit Larry 3 in the file list.

Game blaster
12 voice synthesizer on an 8 byte expansion card half the overall length. You can install the card with the help of a screwdriver. The card contains a 2.5 watt amplifier, a volume control, a stereo outlet (all 12 voices can be directed to the left or the right), jacks for headphones, additional loudspeakers or a stereo system.

The card requires at least 256K of RAM, DOS 2.0, floppy disk drive, CGA, MCGA, EGA or VGA graphic adapter.

Ad-Lib Music Synthesizer Card
The Ad-Lib is an 8 byte expansion card half the overall height of IBM compatible PCs. It has 11 voices and is supported by most manufacturers of games with sound. It features a volume control, headphone jack, and additional outputs for loudspeakers or a stereo system.

Roland MT-32
This card is a professional PC expansion. It supports 32 voices, which actually consist of 8 synthesizers connected to a percussion module. Every synthesizer works on its own MIDI channel (channel 10) to send the rhythm. EASE allows you to compose your own songs. You can also, depending on your system, hook up the Roland MT-32 by cable.

IBM PC Music Feature Card
This expansion card has full overall length. It has 8 voices, uses the FM sound technology and has 240 defined pitches. The user can program 96 additional pitches. The card has a MIDI port that supports devices that comply with MIDI specification 1.0. The card is only available from IBM dealers.

Leisure Suit Larry on the Amiga

Using the Leisure Suit Larry game disks on an Amiga isn't much different
from the PC version. Make backup copies before installing the disks. To be
able to correctly install the copies, they must have the same designation as the
original (i.e., name, label.)

Virus Alert
Larry uses common sense to protect himself from dangerous and deadly viral
infections in his encounters with various people. You should use the same
common sense to protect your computer system from computer viruses located
on disks you insert into your Amiga. If your Leisure Suit Larry is a Sierra
factory original and you break the shrinkwrap yourself, you will never have a
problem.

Computer viruses are self-replicating programs that can destroy your data and
possibly even your hard disk. Virus programs are usually destructive and an
infected system can be a nightmare of lost data and disk crashes. Virus
programmers like to place their destructive virus programs on "pirated" copies
of popular game software. Virus programmers do this so their virus program
will get the widest possible distribution in the shortest time.

Therefore we strongly recommend that you never accept copies of the Larry
games from anyone. Always use backup copies of the original program disks
to start the Larry games! Only use backup copies you have made yourself from
the original program disks. This is the only sure method of protecting your
computer system from a virus infestation. Remember that virus programmers
like to place their nasty programming creations on popular game disks.

Starting Leisure Suit Larry on the Amiga
If you do not have a hard disk and your Amiga has less than 1 meg of memory,
turn your system off and disconnect all external drives. Insert the first disk of
the installed game into the drive DFO: and turn your system on. The Amiga
will now boot from this Leisure Suit Larry disk and you can start playing.

It's a good idea to keep a formatted disk handy to save the game scores. You
should also do this when several players use one Amiga which has a hard disk.

Leisure Suit Larry on the ST

You can operate Leisure Suit Larry games on the ST the same way as you would a PC. First, make backup copies of the original game disks and install the copies.

If you have an Atari 520 ST without any memory expansion, you might have to free up the main memory to make room for the Leisure Suit Larry games. This is done by renaming the Desktop Accessories. The quickest way to do this is to use a different extension, for example .ACX, instead of the normal .ACC extension.

Virus Alert

Larry uses common sense to protect himself from dangerous and deadly viral infections in his encounters with the people he meets. You should use the same common sense to protect your computer system from computer viruses created for the Atari ST. If your Leisure Suit Larry is a Sierra factory original and you break the shrinkwrap yourself, you will never have a problem.

Computer viruses are self-replicating programs that can destroy your data and possibly even your hard disk. Virus programs are usually destructive and an infected system can be a nightmare of lost data and disk crashes. Virus programmers like to place their destructive virus programs on "pirated" copies of popular game software. Virus programmers do this so their virus program will get the widest possible distribution in the shortest time.

Therefore we strongly recommend that you never accept copies of the Larry games from anyone. Always use backup copies of the original program disks to start the Larry games! Only use backup copies you have made yourself from the original program disks. This is the only sure method of protecting your computer system from a virus infestation. Remember virus programmers like to place their nasty programming creations on popular game disks. Protect your important data; practice Safe Computing!

Sound on the ST
Your ST produces better sounding music than that from a PC/compatible. The Sierra games support the internal loudspeaker of the ST. You can use the installation program so that the music of your Leisure Suit Larry games is played on a MIDI device connected to your ST.

The Larry Story ─────────────

Leisure Suit Larry on the Macintosh

The Macintosh provides an excellent implementation of Leisure Suit Larry.
This version of the game contains many useful features, such as accessing
commands by using either pull-down menus or icons. These features save you
time because you don't have to enter all the commands by hand. You can also
use command and control keys to access many of the common commands,
such as "save game", "pause/resume game", and "toggle sound on/off".
Before installing Leisure Suit Larry, you should make backup copies of the
original program disk(s).

Virus Alert
Larry practices Safe Sex to protect himself from dangerous and deadly viral
infections in his encounters with the people he meets. You should practice Safe
Computing to protect your Macintoish from deadly computer viruses. You
never know where a disk has been. If your Leisure Suit Larry is a Sierra
factory original and you break the shrinkwrap yourself, you will never have a
problem.

Computer viruses are self-replicating programs that can destroy your data and
possibly even your hard disk. Virus programs are usually destructive and an
infected system can be a nightmare of lost data and disk crashes. Virus
programmers like to place their destructive virus programs on "pirated" copies
of popular game software. Virus programmers do this so their virus program
will get the widest possible distribution in the shortest time.

Therefore we strongly recommend that you never accept copies of the Larry
games from anyone. Always use backup copies of the original program disks
to start the Larry games! Only use backup copies you have made yourself from
the original program disks. This is the only sure method of protecting your
computer system from a virus infestation. Virus programmers like to place
their nasty programming creations on popular game disks.

Follow the instructions contained in the manual for installing and starting the
Larry games.

Abacus

pc catalog

Order Toll Free 1-800-451-4319

5370 52nd Street SE • Grand Rapids, MI 49512
Phone: (616) 698-0330 • Fax: (616) 698-0325

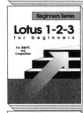

Take Off
With Microsoft Flight Simulator

The most popular flight simulator for your PC and compatible, **Take Off With Microsoft Fl** **Simulator** allows any PC user to simulate flying an aircraft. The *Microsoft Flight Simulator* is just a game; its a true-to-life flight simulation that requires flight knowledge and understand Now you can quickly and easily learn the techniques of operating Flight Simulator to it's ful Whether you are an amateur pilot or a seasoned flying ace this book will teach you how to the most out of flight simulation.

Take Off With Microsoft Flight Simulator teaches you all the useful flight techniques to get in the air quickly and easily. You will learn all about curves, climbing, diving, takeoffs crosswinds, and landing without engines. Whether you're trying to take off and land in Chic in bad weather or just planning to touch down in Red Square, **Take Off With Microsoft Fl** **Simulator** contains all the necessary information you need to become an experienced PC

PC users, pilots and even novices will learn to fly with **Take Off With Microsoft Flight Simula**

Topics include:

✈ *All about Flight Simulator Version 4.0*

✈ *Flight Simulator instrumentation and the different scenarios available*

✈ *Flight techniques: How do I steer this thing?*

✈ *Flight school: Takeoff, climbing, flying on instruments, etc.*

✈ *How to navigate and utilize the autopilot*

✈ *Advanced flight simulations including: Formation flying, multi-player mode, etc.*

✈ *Detailed appendix with card data, map coordinates, technical data and more*

Take Off With Microsoft Flight Simulator is loaded with aviation knowledge you need to ma the skies and become a PC pilot.
ISBN 1-55755-089-1. Suggested Retail Price: $16.95
Available June.